TH RE
OF THE HYDERABAD STATE

Being *The Le Bas Prize* Essay
in the University of Cambridge, 1904.

ROBERT PATON MCAULIFFE

THE NIZAM

THE ORIGIN AND FUTURE OF THE HYDERABAD STATE

Being *The Le Bas Prize* Essay
in the University of Cambridge, 1904.

BY

ROBERT PATON MCAULIFFE
B.A.
Scholar of St. Catherine's College.

DIAMOND BOOKS™
www.diamondbooks.ca

TORONTO, CANADA – 2017

DIAMOND BOOKS - CANADA

DIAMOND BOOKS

Toronto, ON, CANADA

http://www.diamondbooks.ca

BIBLIOGRAPHIC INFORMATION

' THE NIZAM
- THE ORIGIN AND FUTURE OF THE HYDERABAD STATE '
was first published in 1904,
by: C. J. CLAY & SONS, Cambridge University Press,
LONDON.

PUBLISHED IN CANADA

Published in Canada by DIAMOND BOOKS - CANADA, an imprint of DIAMOND PUBLISHERS - http://www.diamondpublishers.com

REPUBLISHED EDITION: August, 2017.

PAPERBACK EDITION : ISBN: 978-1-988942-87-2
E-BOOK EDITION : ISBN: 978-1-988942-86-5

PRINTED IN CANADA

PREFACE.

TO trace the origin of the Hyderabad State is to investigate the stages of a protracted and unfinished evolution. The whole history must be traversed to shew how the State's growth has been spread over centuries of political consolidation. Nor can any period be determined as marking the completion of that process. From the nature of its subject this consideration must be in part an eclectic review of the progress made in one direction; that is, towards the present territorial and political unity of "Le plus grand État Médiatisé" (Reclus, *Géog. Univ.* VIII. 687).

In this work, whatever its value, the writer claims originality, not for historical facts, which are the common property of all who will seek them (although even in these it is hoped some general inaccuracies have been corrected), but for the method and purpose of their selection. The facts narrated have been sought through all the common channels of historical research, and no obligation has been designedly left without acknowledgement in the footnotes or in the appendix, which will be found to contain a list of the chief authorities consulted. It has been thought right to include within this list exponents of conflicting theories, writers whose statements and deductions have been denied or disproved, and a bibliography it is hoped representative of the literature of the subject has been attempted in order that the question may be viewed from more than one aspect.

There is in the writer's knowledge no history published of the Hyderabad State with pretensions to be more than a brief summary or an apologetic statement: but we are fortunate in that there is considerable information dating from before the time when British influence became preponderant, and that this information is often nearly contemporary with the incidents recorded, but especially that, coming down to us through channels and from sources not exclusively British, it escapes the suspicion of having been coloured or manipulated by a British apologist. That it should also be possible to take a fair view of the local history our thanks are due to the conflicting interests that afford accounts and interpretations of events from many varying standpoints, Native, British, French, partisan and impartial.

All these authorities can be conveniently grouped in five classes. In the first are the wide standard histories, from Ferishta to Marshman, which dealing only incidentally with the affairs of Hyderabad enable them to be seen in a right perspective. In this division Gribble's *History of the Deccan* (Vol. I.) may be consulted for the only accessible portrait of the first Asaf Jah, the founder of the reigning house of Hyderabad.

The second group of authorities consists of official publications, treaties, despatches, letters, reports, census notes and gazetteers put forward by authority. It constitutes the raw material of the essayist or, in another aspect, is a storehouse of bare, but indisputable, facts to which appeals can be made. Yet for the historian's purpose this class of documentary evidence needs to be supplemented and interpreted by the personal element of more human authorities. For such a purpose there is exceptional value in the memoirs, speeches, diaries, biographies and historical monographs written by or concerning the Residents and other persons of intimate connexion with the State's history. In them motives, tentative proceedings, and ambitions half attained are revealed in a degree that throws considerable light on the meagre official records.

For the very contrary reason the fourth class is to be carefully investigated. In it are grouped publications of evident partiality such as the pamphlets evoked by the financial scandals or set in circulation by Salar Jang's faction and exploiters to ventilate the Berar grievances. In the same section are the articles to be found in periodical reviews and the more responsible magazines which have opened their sheets to apologetic and polemical writings, for it is a matter of European interest that there are "dans le public anglais sur la façon de considérer la situation matérielle de l'Inde deux *écoles*: l'une vante la prospérité croissante du pays et des habitants, l'autre en dénonce au contraire l'appauvrissement continu" (*Annales des Sciences politiques,* 1903, p. 661).

Finally, there is the class which embraces such legal works as deal with the State's position in the light of International Law or its political relation towards the government of India. These authorities afford the information on which this historical consideration has been made and will (it is thought), if studied in the order indicated, convey the best impression of the history of Hyderabad.

It has not been thought necessary to exhibit a legal refinement in the use of such words as protectorate, suzerainty, feudalism and the like. Writers on the subject of International Law by no means agree in their employment of terms, nor could any satisfactory result be obtained, for the reason that in the language of British diplomacy such technical terms are given values and meanings which they do not bear in the more precise vocabulary of Continental jurists. On this point reference can be made, if desired, to M. Despagnet, *Essai sur les Protectorats*.

It remains to add that in the spelling of Native names it has been recognized that the system invented by Sir W. Hunter and officially accepted (with modifications) is philologically the most correct but is neither consistently employed by its author nor familiar to English readers. The fashion adopted is admittedly arbitrary. In particular the official spelling "Hyderabad" has been preferred to both "Haidarabad" and "Hydrabad": the last form indeed has long been in use, as a matter of convenience, to distinguish the native capital of Sind from its namesake in the Dekhan. The late G. W. Steevens was of opinion that "The only sensible method, it seems, is to spell known names in the way that they are known; others, as you think they look best" (preface, *In India*). The author admits that this has been in the main his principle also.

This Essay was submitted to the Adjudicators of the Le Bas Prize in March 1904. It is now printed unaltered, except that a few corrections have been made, mostly suggested by official reports issued since that date. Advantage has also beeu taken of the opportunity of appending to Chapter I. a valuable paragraph taken from the last Decennial Report on the progress and condition of India.

It should be added that this brief consideration was intended to be nothing more than an Essay. It should be judged as an attempt, by one with limited time to give to the subject and with no personal knowledge of India, to investigate and understand a chapter of Indian history. Looked at so, this Essay it is hoped may be thought to fulfil the intentions of the founders of the Le Bas Prize and be a contribution to the study of "the history, institutions and probable destinies and prospects of the Anglo-Indian Empire."

S. Catharine's College, Cambridge.
Easter Term, 1904.

CONTENTS

THE NIZAMS OF HYDERABAD*.

1. *Nizam-ul-Mulk* (1713—1748).
Known also by his name Mir Kamrudin Khan,
by his earliest and most common title Chin Kalich Khan,
by the titles also of Asaf Jah and Fath Jang Nizam-ud-Daula:
chief minister to Muhammad Shah,
Subahdar of the Dekhan.

- *Ghazi-ud-din Khan.*
  He was absent from the Dekhan till 1752, and then in trying to take the Subahdari from Salabat Jang he died, perhaps poisoned. See Hollingberry, *Nizam Alee Khaun*, p. 49.
- 2. *Nasir Jang.* 1748—1750.
  - 3. *Muzaffar Jang.* Dec. 1750—Jan. 1751.
    A grandson of Nizam-ul-Mulk by a favourite daughter. He fell in the hour he won the Nizamat.
- 4. *Salabat Jang.* 1750—1761.
  Deposed in 1761 by Nizam Ali and murdered in 1763.
- 5. *Nizam Ali,* Nizam-ul-Mulk, Asaf Jah. 1761—1803.
  - 6. *Sikandar Shah.* 1803—1829.
    - 7. *Nasir-ud-Daula.* 1829—1857.
      The Salar Jang appointed Minister in 1853.
      - 8. *Afzal-ud-Daula.* 1857—1869
        - His Highness
          9. *Mir Mahbub Ali Khan,* Bahadur Fath Jang, Nizam-ud-Daula, Nizam-ul-Mulk, GCSI, etc., etc.
          Succeeded 1869 at age of 3: invested with full powers 1884.
- *Basalat Jang.*

* I am indebted for the scheme to Mr Sewell's *Sketch of the Dynasties of Southern India*, p. 35 (1883).

CHAPTER I.

INTRODUCTORY. MEDIÆVAL HISTORY. THE ENTRANCE OF THE TRADING COMPANIES.

TWO-THIRDS of the Indian Empire are composed of the Native protected States, whose reigning Princes are in various forms of subordinate alliance with the Emperor, or in the official, but, owing to the danger of a false analogy, less appropriate phrase, under his suzerainty[1].

Though not decisive, it is instructive to find that Sir George Campbell concludes in his *Modern India* that of these Nepal alone possesses any remains of independence[2]. It has been more recently stated that there exist in India "des États protégés ou feudataires dont l'indépendance est plus ou moins reconnue par des traités, illusoire presque toujours dans l'application[3]," and this sentence admirably sums up the history of the Hyderabad State, which of all the native States, forming 364 distinct units, is the premier in importance and in size.

[1] Ilbert, *Gov. of India*, p. 456.

[2] See also M. Chailley-Bert, *Les Prot. de l'Inde Brit.*

[3] *Précis de Géographie Écon.*, Dubois et Kergomard, 1903.

In area as large as Italy the Nizam's dominions[1] constitute a vast sloping plateau of mean elevation, comprising the heart of the Dekhan. Northward, separated from the dominions by a mountain chain, but still, as no part of British India, included in them, lies Berar or the Hyderabad Assigned Districts, with an area larger than that of Denmark, and known locally as Varhad or Barad. A study of the map will shew that the dominions, now entirely defined by British territory, touch on all sides what have been inflammable points in the geography of Indian history.

Primarily they have been collected from the territories of great Aryan nations resident in Telingana, Karnatika, Maharashtra, and Gondwana.

The history of these countries before the misnamed Mughal invasion has little credit, but the broad statements can be laid down that while the Muhammadans were entering Europe through Spain, their coreligionists invaded Hindustan from the northwest through Sind, and that the subsequent three centuries of Afghan rule were marked by the steady expansion of the Muslim power established at Delhi, until under their second dynasty the Muhammadans entered the Dekhan. The south country as far north as the Narbada had been subject to Rajput princes whose seat was in the strong and ancient fortress of Deogiri, Ptolemy's Tagara, where at the close of the 13th century A.D. Ramdeo (or Ramachandra, for there are both names found) was reigning as Raja of

[1] See *Asia*, Vol. ii., by A. H. Keene, F.R.G.S. Exclusive of Berar, Hyderabad contains over 80,000 sq. miles.

Maharashtra, and, in the eyes of the Muslims, King of the Dekhan. In 1306 he came into conflict with the Imperial power for withholding the tribute for the previous three years and was compelled to capitulate on the approach of the Emperor's servant Malik Kafur with an overwhelming force. He and his successors remained tributaries of the Emperor until in the reign of the mad Muhammad Tughlak the empire began to be dismembered. It was then that in 1347 Hasan Gangu, an Afghan of the lowest rank, founded in the Dekhan the Bahmani empire, out of which in the early years of the 16th century the famous five Shahi kingdoms were cut, as in turn the great governors asserted their rebellious independence.

Of these Sultan Kutb Kuli Khan, a Turkman adventurer from Persia, who had risen in the Bahmani service to be governor of Telingana, was independent in all but name from 1512 A.D., when he founded at Golkonda the dynasty that bears his name. At the time of his murder in 1543 his territory extended from the Godavari beyond the Kistna and from the sea to about the seventy-eighth degree of longitude west of the present city of Hyderabad.

To that city its builder, Muhammad Kuli, fifth in descent from Kutb Shah, gave on its foundation in 1589 the name of Bhagnagar, "The Fortunate City," in honour of his mistress, Bhagmati, renaming it at her death Hyderabad, after Hyder Allah, the Lion of God, the Khalif Ali. But the city did not for yet many years supplant the older fortress of Golkonda as the seat of government. Entering into the usual Muhammadan alliances, during a long and successful reign marked by conquest and splendour for thirty-four years Muhammad Kuli extended his realms at the expense of his Hindu neighbours. Such, briefly but necessarily told, is the story of the original kingdoms from which the Nizam's dominions were to be shaped.

In the following reign the Mughals under Shah Jahan appeared in the Dekhan on their ill-advised policy of premature expansion, and the history proper of Hyderabad commences. Already Akbar had so extended his rule that Berar, then including all the present subah of Aurangabad, was in his hands from 1596 until his death. In Muhammadan days it had been a province under the immediate control of the Imperial legate; in the time of the Bahmani kings it appears as a troublesome border province with ill-defined frontiers, and after several vicissitudes was finally constituted by Akbar an Imperial subah.

At a very early period of his desultory operations Shah Jahan had overawed Abdalla Kutb Shah, of Golkonda, had exacted a regular tribute, and forbidden the Shiite practice of reciting in the public prayer during the Friday Khotab the name of the King of Persia. A peculiar sequence of events connected with the intrigues of his Persian Minister Mir Jumla[1], whom Bernier calls "a man of almost unimaginable capacity," brought him to more abject dependence. Dying in 1672 a tributary of Delhi he

[1] He instigated, for private reasons, Aurangzeb to take Golkonda as the surest road to the throne of his father; cf. Sleeman, *Rambles and Recollections*, 1—360.

was succeeded by his son-in-law Abu Husain who, following the custom of the illiterate Muhammadan princes, entrusted his affairs to one of the professional Brahman class, a Maratha, on whose advice he entered into rebellious alliance with the Marathas, bringing on Hyderabad pillage and burning, and to himself deposition and lifelong imprisonment as a protector of infidels. He was the last of the princes of Golkonda preceding the Asafia dynasty, known in European history as the Nizams of Hyderabad[1], who were in the disintegration effected by the fitful wars of Aurangzeb to constitute themselves with the other Imperial lieutenants independent and hereditary sovereigns. Even at this period the foreign trading companies had entered into relations with the King of Golkonda. For some years the Portuguese had maintained a factory at San Thomé, within his dominions, but in 1662 the town had passed out of their hands into the possession of a Muslim power dependent on Golkonda. About ten years earlier the traveller Bernier, who from his position as the Imperial physician was thoroughly versed in Indian affairs, had advised the French Company to procure factories within the kingdom of Golkonda and at Masulipatam, as well as in Bengal; and in December 1699 the French agent at Surat, a certain Marcara, was able in spite of opposition from the English and the Dutch to procure a firman from the king permitting the French Company to trade in all his dominions and establish a post at Masulipatam.

[1] The title is perhaps first officially employed, with definite local meaning, in the confirmatory treaty of 1831.

They were also especially exempted from taxes on both imports and exports. Pursuing the advantage gained, the French commander De la Haye assaulted and captured San Thomé in 1672, and successfully resisted the attempt of the King of Golkonda to eject him. Negotiations for the peaceful tenure of the town were thwarted by the English traders, and soon afterwards the Dutch, who in Europe were at war with France, joined the king in ejecting the invaders. Other commercial settlements were made between the French Company and the native prince, but it was not until the advent of Pierre Benoît Dumas that the connexion with Golkonda, and its successor Hyderabad, became political. Yet it is well to mention these early relations with Golkonda inasmuch as their common omissiou in historical narratives obscures a stage of the State's development, and fails to shew the sequence of intervention by the trading companies, if, as is the general practice, the first appearance of the Companies is indicated as occurring upon the death of the first Nizam of Hyderabad.

The founder of the dynasty of the Nizams was Abid Kuli Khan, once Kazi of Bokhara, a lineal descendant of the first Khalif. During the reign of Shah Jahan he had entered India and Aurangzeb's service. After winning a name as a brilliant general, in 1686 at the siege of Golkonda, where his descendants were to reign, he "drank," the native historian writes, "the sherbet of death from the hands of the Almighty's messenger," but his grandson Mir Kamrudin, known better by the title of Chin Kalich

Khan, was a most successful opportunist, clear-sighted and patient[1], who entering into the combination that after two short reigns placed Farrukh Siyyar on the throne of Delhi[2] was appointed Viceroy of the Dekhan with the ancient title of Nizam-ul-Mulk Bahadur (Lord Regulator of the State), and in that capacity reduced to order the territories known as the northern Sarkars. At the dissolution of the Bahmani Empire these dominions fell under the rule of the Kutb Shahi State of Golkonda, but since the destruction of that State's sovereignty by the Mughals had enjoyed a turbulent independence in the anarchy pervading the Dekhan. In later times they became an important element in the political question, so that their connexion with Hyderabad calls for a brief notice at this early period.

The new Emperor was the instrument of his creators and ministers, the brothers Sayyid, and in endeavouring to form a coalition of the military nobility against them he effected his own deposition and execution.

Through the stormy next six months that were ended by the accession of Muhammad Shah (1719–1748), Chin Kalich Khan was with the power behind the throne, but disappointed in the partition of honours and suspected of too great an eminence by the brothers Sayyid, he turned with large forces from his new governorship of Malwa to the Dekhan and

[1] He was for a short time Subahdar of Oudh, but retired to live for a while as a Fakir in Delhi until better days came.

[2] By the battle of Agra Dec. 28, 1712. Four days later he took formal possession.

establishing himself at Asirghar maintained his position against the forces of the Emperor's masters, whom a court conspiracy shortly afterwards cut off. To the vacant office of Chief Minister at Delhi Chin Kalich Khan was summoned, and after securing practical independence in the Dekhan, he proceeded early in 1722 to assume his office, only to be "alienated from the mind of the Emperor[1]" by a cabal, and to retire in consequence to his viceroyalty in the Dekhan in October 1723 with the title of Supreme Deputy of the Empire. It was more than a suspicion that the unsuccessful attempt of the local governor of Hyderabad to dispossess the Viceroy was directly inspired by the Emperor, who at the same time removed the Nizam from his subsidiary governorships of Malwa and Guzerat. The incident, for it was nothing more, strengthened the Nizam in his independence. It was then, according to the most credible narrative, that to cover his failure the Emperor honoured his Viceroy with the title of Asaf Jah[2], and with instructions "to settle the country, repress the turbulent, punish the rebels, and cherish the people."

Conflicting accounts ascribe to various dates the presentation of this title, by which the dynasty of the Nizams is still locally known, but, whatever the occasion, it is evident that during this period it was held with nothing more than a delegated and viceregal authority. And although the seat of admini-

[1] Native historian.

[2] *i.e.*, Equal to Asaf, the reputed Grand Vizier of King Solomon.

stration was at first established at Aurangabad, and later removed further from the Maratha border to Hyderabad, that city did not become the recognized capital until the time of Salabat, while even now the Nizam is regarded, by convention, merely as encamped in the Dekhan, not established in a permanent palace. Neither did the founder of the kingdom ever assume the title or insignia of royalty, nor his successors when invited consent to do so, or to dispense with the formal confirmation of their office by the Mughal Emperors and their successors. It was only that the retention of the choicest piece of Imperial patronage became hereditary in the family of Chin Kalich Khan, whose immunity in his virtual independence was due to the consideration that he was the only barrier to the insurgent Marathas. Their activity, however, it remained his policy to divert from himself to Delhi, until their ambitions, as enunciated by Baji Rao,—"Let us strike the withered trunk and the branches will fall of themselves[1]," became a personal menace and drove him into active support of the Emperor, to lose all his territories from the Narbada to the Chambal, including Malwa, to which he had been restored. Yet in spite of its object the Maratha enterprise had a moulding, compressing, unifying influence on Hyderabad.

In 1741 the Nizam was found again at the Emperor's side, but being recalled from participation in the turmoil of the Persian invasion, concerning

[1] Elphinstone, *H. of India*, ii. 599.

his part in which Dow's *Hindostan* affords much curious information, he took advantage of his son's revolt to consolidate his possessions south of the Narbada, and to reduce the Karnatik to the status of an hereditary province, while leading the prevailing faction of Turani nobles at the Court of Delhi, where he was represented by his eldest son; for he neither severed his connexion with the Emperor nor disclaimed his own subordination. In correspondence passing between him and the French at Pondichery in 1741 he was accorded merely the position of chief Minister of Muhammad Shah, and claimed no more[1], although the tone of his letters to the French governor was distinctly condescending. Not the least interesting feature of this communication is the prominence of the title Asaf Jah, which clearly is meant (the Emperor being described as another Solomon) to mark the premier rank of the Nizam among the Imperial officers.

At the time of his death he was ruling over all the present State, and, as the titular subahdar, over all Southern India. In reality his sphere of power was defined by the Bhonsla northwards, and on the south by the Rajas of Mysore, Trichinopoli, and smaller principates. Even his most immediate vassal, the Raja of Arcot, Lord of the Karnatik, acted in complete independence, and it was he who received at Madras and Pondichery, as humble traders paying tribute and rent, the English and French adventurers who were to intervene in Hyderabadi

[1] See letter in Abbé Guyon: *Hist. des Indes Orient.* (1744).

politics[1]. With the Nizam's death in 1748 came the usual struggles over the succession. His second son Nasir Jang seizing the treasury drew the army to him, alleging a renunciation on his elder brother's part. Another claimant appeared in Muzaffar Jang, a grandson, claiming succession by bequest. As an Imperial legate only, it is to be noticed, the Nizam could bequeath by Muhammadan law neither sovereignty nor treasure, and it was here that the European power intervened at the close of the medieval period of South India, at a time also when, with the Mughal Empire in decadence, a wave of Hindu enthusiasm drove those "patrons of anarchy," the Marathas, over the whole peninsula.

It was nearly two hundred years since in 1583 Ralph Fitch and others "being desirous to see the countreys of the East India" first came to Golkonda[2]. Their successors the East India Companies of France and England were almost the last of the adventurous

[1] The first communications between the English Co. and the Nizam were opened by Commodore Griffin commanding the naval forces of Madras. He successfully appealed against the French proclivities of the governor of Arcot.

[2] For an account of how Ralph Fitch of London, merchant, John Newberie, William Leedes, jeweller, and James Story, painter, were imprisoned at Goa and escaped to Golkonda, see Hakluyt's *Collection of the Early Voyages, Travels and Discoveries*, etc., 1810 ed., vol. ii. 382.

"Hence wee went for Gulconda the king whereof is called Cutup de lashach. Here and in the kingdome of Hidalcan and in the countrey of the King of Decan bee the Diamants found of the olde water."

The king mentioned is Muhammad Kuli Kutb Shah, the founder of Bhagnagar, *i.e.* Hyderabad.

corporations to trade with the East Indies. Between them there was, until Aurangzeb died, little of the hostility that marked the relations of other Companies, but at his death the French adventurers took advantage of the general anarchy with no small additions to their factories and *prestige*, so that the opening of the 18th century saw a political, if not commercial, French supremacy.

M. Dumas, their governor of Pondichery, by intervention in local quarrels initiated the policy of alliance and protectorate that was more fully elaborated by his brilliant successor Joseph François Dupleix. It was in Lord Macaulay's phrase, modelled on M. Hamont's, "to govern the motions and speak through the mouth of some glittering puppet dignified with the title of Nabob or Nizam." The war breaking out in Europe over the question of the Austrian Succession was welcome in the East, and when concluded by the treaty of Aix-la-Chapelle in 1748, left the French *prestige* heightened in India, where the international relations of England and France afforded an opportunity for the prosecution of informal hostilities on the earliest occasions. Such an occasion presented itself the very year of the treaty, for the Nizam-ul-Mulk who ruled from the Narbada to Trichinopoli, from Masulipatam to Bijapur, was dead with no heir-apparent either by Muhammadan law or by that of the Asafia House. For Hyderabad and the English the situation was more critical than could have been then evident. For Hyderabad it was the beginning of a new evolution to end in the formation of the present State.

The British policy will be found beginning from this crisis to pass through four stages. First of all the maintenance of a balance of power was sought; then (and here begins the first of Sir William Lee-Warner's three divisions of the history) the position of "*primus inter pares,*" followed by that of "*primus supra omnes,*" until finally there was entertained the project of domination, to be reached by the realisation of the successive theories of the Ring Fence, Subsidiary Alliance, Subordinate Isolation, Protectorate, and Real Union[1]. As an introduction to the second chapter of Hyderabadi history there may well be quoted a most valuable paragraph from the last Decennial Report on the Progress of India. The whole chapter is most interesting[2]. It calls attention to two striking facts, "First, that with remarkably few exceptions these States, certainly in their present dimensions, rank and position, are of more recent origin than the British Power in India. Secondly, that had it not been for the protecting arm of that Power there is hardly a single State that would not have long since been absorbed by a more powerful neighbour or dismembered by fratricidal rivalry or internal sedition. The rise of the greater number of the States in the north and centre of the country took place during the decadence of the Moghal Empire and the general anarchy and confusion that prevailed everywhere in India during the last half of

[1] The whole thought is from M. Chailley-Bert, *Les Protect. de l'Inde Brit.* i. Sec. 3.

[2] Statement:—East India (*Progress and Condition,* 1901–2), pp. 23, 24.

the 18th century and attended the downfall of the Maratha rule in the early years of the 19th. We thus find in power descendants of the successful freebooter, the favoured minister or general, and the rebellious deputy of his Sovereign." It proceeds to say that the relations between the British Government and the Native States have been clearly described by Sir William Lee-Warner, and quotes his words concerning the three periods into which the history falls:—

"Each period is the expression of an idea, which has left its mark as much on the form and language of the treaties as upon their extent and their objects. Up to the year 1813, which may be fixed as the closing year of the first period, the pressure of Parliament and the prudence of the Merchant Company operated in the direction of a policy of non-intervention. The Company was barely struggling for its existence, and it recoiled from the expense and danger of extending its treaties of alliance and self-defence beyond the Ring Fence of its own territorial acquisitions. In the next period, which lasted from 1814 to the Mutiny of 1857, larger schemes of Empire dawned upon its horizon and dominated the policy of its Governor-Generals. The exclusion of any States from the Protectorate was proved by experience to be both impolitic and cowardly. Empire was forced upon the British rulers of India, and the bitter fruits of a policy of leaving the States unprotected were gathered in the Pindari War, in the revival of schemes of conquest in the minds of the Mahratta, and in the humiliation of the Rajput Houses. Surrounded on all sides by the country princes, the Company's officers saw that no alternative remained except annexation, which they wished to avoid, or a thorough political settlement of the Empire step by step with the extension of their direct rule. Without order on their frontier, peace in their own territories was impossible; and the only prospect of order among the Native States was to undertake arbitration in all their disputes with each other, and to deprive all alike of the right to make war or to enter into any unauthorised conventions with each other. The policy of the period was one of isolating the Native States, and subordinating them to the political ascendancy of the British power. The expressions of 'mutual alliance' and 'reciprocal agreement' are exchanged for the phrases 'subordinate alliance,' 'protection,' and 'subordinate co-operation.' But whilst the States are deprived of all control over their external relations, the traditional policy of non-interference is still for a while preserved in their internal affairs. Here the phrases of international law maintain their last stronghold, and it is deemed inconsistent with a sovereignty to introduce a foreign agency for effecting any reforms. No remedy for continued misrule is yet known except a declaration of war, or, at a later date, annexation. At last a further change occurs—with the suppression of the Mutiny 'the Crown of England stands forth the unquestioned ruler in all India.' Annexation is found to be needlessly drastic. International law is wholly out of place, and the new conception of Indian sovereignties not only justifies, but requires, intervention to save the State. A different set of engagements are taken, which bring to light the union of the States with the British Government in the extension of railways and in the common promotion of works of public benefit. The relations which to-day subsist between the protected States and their protector are the resultant of these three periods, and of these several ideas, namely, non-intervention, subordinate isolation, union[1]."

[1] Sir W. Lee-Warner, KCSI., *The Protected Princes of India*, quoted in the Government Report.

CHAPTER II.

THE FRENCH AND ENGLISH DUEL. SUBSIDIARY ALLIANCE. THE CONTINGENT. INTERNAL PROTECTORATE.

THE situation in the dispute of the succession has been stated. It was complicated by the appearance of a claimant to the feudatory throne of the Karnatik, and the adoption of opposing interests by the English and French Companies. After some successes and many intrigues the English candidate, Nasir Jang, was murdered in a plot of Dupleix's laying by his own Patan nawabs (Dec. 5, 1750), and Muzaffar Jang succeeded, with Dupleix paramount as king-maker and suzerain. Of Muzaffar Jang it is said that "Il était condamné à n'être jamais qu'une pompeuse marionnette dans les mains de politiques[1]," and a body of French troops was stationed under the Marquis de Bussy in Hyderabad itself, which was at Bussy's suggestion made the capital in 1753, to protect and intimidate the Nizam. For its maintenance the cession of large territories near Pondichery,

[1] Hamont's *Dupleix*, p. 28.

the province of Karikal, and the district of Masulipatam were demanded, and so was commenced a practice that became a vital condition of the State's existence and is the chief subject of this consideration. The violent death of the new Nizam in 1751 was followed by the selection by the French of a successor even more subservient, in the person of Salabat Jang; but it is more important to note the anxiety growing in Europe at the continuous and unauthorised hostilities between the French and the English Companies, resulting in the withdrawal of their author Dupleix, "the Alberoni of the East," and in M. Godeheu's peace mission that negotiated the provisional treaty of Pondichery in 1754. Its first and chief article, that both nations should for ever cease from interference in the differences of native Princes, was not likely to be long respected by either contracting party: it was, in Hamont's epigram, the substitution of Augustulus for Caesar, and the renunciation of the French methods and ideals that had dominated India.

After five years the treaty of Aix-la-Chapelle was indeed honoured with eighteen months' truce, but there was no promise of ultimate peace in the thought that while the French were paramount at the Court of the Nizam, whose precarious throne they were pledged by the acceptance of territorial security to maintain, the English Company were in a like position at the Court of his vassal in the Karnatik. Both were deeply committed, and from this time the English Company's policy became timidly aggressive.

The official renewal of war in Europe over the Austrian Succession was made an excuse for intervention in the dispute of the Nizamat, and more directly, for sending from France the Irish Comte de Lally with a force for which Dupleix had begged in vain. He landed in India, as he writes in his letters, "pour en chasser les Anglais," and not otherwise to continue Dupleix's policy. The subsequent private and public quarrels of Bussy and Lally, aggravated by the latter's evil genius, Père Lavaur, by endangering the French territories, already menaced by Clive, compelled the withdrawal of Bussy with his subsidiary force from Hyderabad, and made the weakness of the Nizam's position resting solely on French support apparent to all, and most clearly to the Nizam. Not the least of his dangers was the attitude of his brother Ali, in whom was early seen, by the Mughalai party at Court, a counterpoise to the development of French ambitions at the cost of Muhammadan supremacy. Their opposition to such a project had in 1756 been so clearly seen that Bussy seized Hyderabad, while Ali had been alternately appeased with honours and restricted by supervision. In 1757 he was formally invested as heir to the succession and entitled Nizam-ul-Mulk, Asaf Jah, which serves to remind English readers that these familiar titles were no distinguishing prerogative of the reigning prince, although by habituation they have become so understood and officially employed. Suspicious of his treatment, Nizam Ali revolted in some degree and occupied the capital, but acknowledging his brother's supremacy was entrusted with almost equal authority.

In the meantime, on the invitation of the chief local prince in the Sarkars, Colonel Forde had been despatched from Calcutta, stormed Masulipatam and gained for the East India Company all the territory dependent on that fortress, thus transferring to the Company the dominating influence in Hyderabad, which was marked by the first treaty with the Nizam in 1759. By it the French troops at the capital and on the coast were to be expelled for ever, but the northern Sarkars were in practice mainly left to the nominal rule of the Nizam.

In retrospect it is seen that it was the effort of the French to impose their authority over the Dekhani dependencies, especially in the disposal of the Nawabship of the Karnatik, that enabled the English Company to acquire in five years nearly all the territories their rivals had ever held, and to exercise a preponderant, if not predominant, influence in the Nizam's councils, although over His Highness they claimed with wise patience no suzerainty for yet thirty-five years. It is a curious fact that at this time Clive foretold the later policy of England towards India in a letter to Pitt (dated Jan. 7, 1759), in which he suggested the means and pointed out the advantages of the assumption by the Crown of an absolute government. The proposition was however laid aside for a century, till 1858, when it was embodied in the proclamation of November 5th.

In 1761 Bussey's forecast and the Nizam's persistent apprehensions of his brother were realized: Nizam Ali superseded and imprisoned the Nizam, on the pretext of detected communications in time of war with the Marathas, and two years later was participant in his murder. Following the procedure of Salabat with the French in 1752, Nizam Ali now ten years later offered the English Company four of the Northern Sarkars in return for armed assistance; but the offer could not be entertained. In October, 1765, however, the directors were advised that on the initiative of Mr Palk, president of Fort St George, *Sanads* for all five Sarkars had been obtained from the Emperor, "that mysterious fountain from which his strongest neighbour might pretend to draw authority[1]," against a possible revival of French activity in the old theatre of the Coromandel wars. In strict legality the Sarkars were subordinate to the Nizam as Viceroy: that had been recognized by the treaty of Paris two years earlier, but more remotely they were subject to the Emperor of Delhi. In the name of the Company military possession was taken, nor was the Nizam's position as the intermediate over-lord acknowledged until his retaliatory raid of the following year into the country of the Company's ally, the Nawab of the Karnatik, made it expedient to obtain his acquiescence to a treaty by which the Company in return for a ratification of their grant of the Sarkars agreed to keep a subsidiary force at his disposal for any duty "right and proper" of which the Company were to be the entire and sole

[1] Westlake, *Chapters on International Law*, p. 201.

judges[1], and when their services were not required to pay annually certain benevolences in consideration of the free gift of the Sarkars. The life interest of the Nizam's brother in the fifth, the Gantur, Sarkar with final reversion to the Company was admitted. The Nizam and the Company were to have friends and enemies in common. In the course of the political developments there should be noticed the implication of the Nizam's independence in foreign politics of the dictation of the Emperor, but it cannot be said that in this the Company's advisers followed an invariable and consistent policy.

The most important feature of this treaty is perhaps beneath the surface. So far the policy of the Ring-Fence had prevailed. That was the maintenance of a circle of protection, or in other words, the establishment of the frontier protectorate. It began after the victory of Plassey and lasted until the end of Lord Minto's term of office, being broken only by Lord Wellesley during that period, in which annexation was discountenanced, treaties of alliance rare. But by the treaty of Nov. 12, 1766, with Hyderabad, a new system was inaugurated. Once again Hyderabad is shewn as the field of political experiments. It was felt that the barriers set up were not firm, could not be strengthened and must be replaced. The theory of Subsidiary Alliance was developed. Equality gave place to superiority as an ideal, and frontier protectorates such as Hyderabad became in anticipation dependent and controlled

[1] Articles 2 and 10, Nov. 12, 1766.

dominions, although the word protectorate was probably unknown and the idea but in the kernel at this period. It required the treaties of 1798 to define more exactly the situation accepted in 1766.

An opportunity of putting into practice the terms of the treaty presented itself the following year. Hyder Naik at the head of a mercenary band had usurped the throne of his master, the Hindu Raja, and aimed with French encouragement at making Mysore the paramount power in South India. It necessitated the hasty, but legal, withdrawal from Hyderabad of the English protecting forces, to the displeasure of the Nizam, who for a while joined "the rebel and usurper," as he afterwards styled him in the treaty of reconciliation (Madras 1768)[1]. By this treaty an arrangement was effected to "bury in oblivion what is past" and to release the Nizam from his former liability to furnish the Company with troops on their demand. But the article of greatest interest and importance in consideration of later diplomacy is the sixth. It provided the Nizam at his need and charges, *whenever the situation would allow*, with Sepoys, artillery, and European gunners, and thus foreshadowed that subsidiary system which Warren Hastings evolved with real genius. Of the Subsidiary Alliance there is no better description than in the following sentences:—"Cette alliance a débuté par fournir aux princes indigènes des secours militaires; elle a continué par former à la discipline européenne leurs contingents indigènes qui assisteront

[1] Article 9. The Nizam "declares and makes known to the world that he regards the said Naigue as a rebel and usurper."

les Anglais; puis par demander, au lieu de secours en hommes, des secours en argent; puis par faire assigner des terres comme garantie des sommes promises. Propriétaires ou possesseurs de ces terres, il a fallu dès lors, les défendre. De là toute l'évolution de la politique britannique[1]."—It was the determination of Warren Hastings not to permit a Maratha reign of terror to build up another political unity out of the vacated dominion of the Mughals, and with this thought he bound by treaties and subsidies the native princes in a form of Subsidiary Alliance that secured the integrity of their realms, while placing them in a dependent relationship to the Company, and drawing to the latter the allegiance that was due to the nominal Emperor, for the acceptance of a subsidiary force gave the British as "an indispensable correlative of the stipulation for protection[2]" a controlling power in all external and, in some degree, internal policy. The Mughal Empire, in fact, and the Maratha were but terms: they were no longer even territorial aggregates. They had never been administrative unities. The Vizier in Oudh, the Nizam at Hyderabad, the Mayor of the Palace at Puna, asserted or denied at pleasure their submission to the puppet kings at Delhi and Satara. In Macaulay's phrase the form and the power of government were everywhere separated; and with a splendid disregard of consistency, either party for the advantage of the moment advocated the claim

[1] *Annales des sciences politiques*, 1899, p. 154 note. Prinsep, *H. of India*, vol. i. p. 5, can be seen also.

[2] Prinsep, *H. of India*, vol. i. p. 5.

of the actual or the titular government. It is doubtful whether throughout India one single State possessed the double authority.

This manipulation of political theories was especially seen in the relations of the English Company with the Hyderabad State, for they counteracted the native States with their own diplomatic weapons.

Meanwhile in the uncertain position of the Sarkars there was the assurance of future trouble. The benevolences due for them, according to the conditions of the Company's tenure, had fallen into arrears and desuetude, and further, an illegal arrangement had been made by the Madras Government with the Nizam's brother, by which he leased to the Company the Gantur Sarkar in which he held a life-interest. It had been done with no sanction from Bengal and was immediately disowned by the Supreme Government, as constituting an unfriendly act against the Nizam of the nature of an intrigue with his subjects; and its chief authors including the Governor, Sir William Rumbald, were punished. But it had the double effect of driving His Highness into hostile coalition with the Marathas, and of occasioning the mission of the first political agent, Mr Hollond, to the Nizam's Court. The conciliatory action of the Supreme Government in the restoration of the Sarkar, over which so much trouble had been made, was reciprocated by the Nizam, influenced by his now dominant wish for an ultimate alliance with the Company, and a negotiation was almost effected for the rendition of the Sarkar in perpetuity when advices from England forbade such a course[1]. In this the Company's policy was more clearly shewn in 1786, when Lord Cornwallis went to India with explicit instructions to demand the surrender of the Sarkar, which by the extinction of the life-interest of Basalat Jang had legally reverted to the Company four years before. These instructions could not be immediately executed when English and French relations were critical, but two years later the demand was made and, being at once accorded, became the occasion of the first appointment of a political Resident to the Hyderabad Court, to secure compliance with treaty obligations. In this connexion, the question of the Sarkars is of primary importance for any appreciation of the manner in which the English supremacy grew up and shaped the fortunes of the State. It bound the two Powers together by a tie of preferential treatment, and as it was felt that such marks of preference for English friendship should be the occasion of a closer bond, an ingenious and happy expedient was found (in view of the legal prohibition of any contraction of new alliances not arising from war) of considering the old treaty of 1768 as still binding while interpreting and defining it in such a manner as to satisfy the Nizam's requirements. The expression that the subsidiary force should be at the Nizam's disposal whenever the situation allowed, was defined as meaning that

[1] Negotiations were opened, during the war in 1784, with Nizam Ali, and it was purposed to cede His Highness all the Northern Sarkars, but Lord Macartney who had arrived at Madras procured the withdrawal of the scheme.

the force should always be available except against the Company's allies, among whom were specified the Maratha chiefs; but the name of Tipu Sultan was not on the exceptive lists.

It was further laid down, that either party should be at liberty to pursue diplomatic communications with any other of the Dekhani powers for its private benefit, provided such intercourse was not hostile to its ally, but an explicit refusal to reopen the question of the Northern Sarkars was given. Throughout history this latter decision has never been rescinded.

This interpretation of the treaty was conveyed in a letter from the Governor-General (July 7, 1789), who was in a position to inform the Nizam that the letter had, by a declaration of the British Parliament, all the force of law. For the opinion had been growing in England, that so vast an empire could not be held by a trading Company, and the question becoming one of party politics a Board of Control to ratify or annul the Company's political actions was constituted, thus bringing the Nizam's Government into direct and permanent relation for the first time with the British Crown. But the domination of the Marathas over Hyderabadi affairs ceased only when "*Citizen*" Tipu of Mysore bought peace in 1792 at the cost of half his territory, at the close of a vain attempt to disestablish a balance of power in which the Company's intervention could always turn the scale. In the division of Tipu's surrendered dominions the Nizam participated. A little later he was involved in a dispute with the Marathas of

Puna over certain lands and revenues, and on his request that the British subsidiary force, with which he was conditionally supplied, should be augmented and made available for offensive purposes, he was informed that from any intervention, other than mediatorial, the Governor-General, Sir John Shore (afterwards Lord Teignmouth), claimed legal exemption by the express terms of the definitive letter of 1789 which prohibited the employment of the force against the Marathas, and although the Resident, Sir John Kennaway, wrote (Jan. 1, 1794) that the Nizam was ready to enter into engagements such as would render the English "masters of his country for ever," the position did not invite a closer alliance that might bring with it governmental responsibilities but no commercial advantage to a trading company. At this neutrality the Nizam had resort to his domestic levies under the general command of M. Raymond. In addition to the Corps François de Raymond[1] he possessed other mercenaries commanded by American, French, and Irish officers. But of all these Raymond's Corps was the chief. It formed the main part of the Nizam's army, was paid from territorial assignments, and being commanded by Frenchmen "of the most virulent and notorious principles of Jacobinism," was the basis of the French party in India. The ensuing battle of Kardla was one of mercenaries led by the European adventurers to be found during these years at every

[1] Cf. Fraser, *Our Faithful Ally*, etc. p. 147. Raymond affected to consider his corps "a French body of troops employed and subsidized by the Nizam."

native Court, and significant of the fact that the native thrones could only stand with alien support. It had not indeed been decided by a pacific Court of Directors that in the Nizam's case this support should solely be the Company's, but in that direction the future looked, and the terrors of the socialistic and revolutionary opinions of the French at home and in India were made to strike with full force into the Nizam, above all things orientally conservative.

During the unhappy movements of this war, the tranquillity of the Nizam's dominions had been secured according to treaty by the Company, but Sir John Shore's neutrality was bitter, and an attempt was made to dispense with the Company's battalions while the French force was enlarged into an excellent and formidable corps. For a few days the battalions were dismissed[1], and the course of history might have been very different had not immediate local and family reasons necessitated their recall, for even if their use could not be permitted against the Marathas so as to disturb the judicious political balance obtained in the Dekhan, they gave the Nizam both importance and security. At the same time their retention was desirable to the Company as protecting the Karnatik, and affording an entry into Mysore, Berar, the countries of the Peshwa, and in particular of Sindhia, who through the Maratha dissensions now loomed far greater in the political outlook than the Peshwa or the Nizam. There was the further consideration that while Tipu Sultan was inviting the Nizam into a combination

[1] Quite legally by clause 4 of the Definitive Letter of 1789.

against the British, and extending even to Arabia his correspondence to effect such a Jihad, the English faction at Hyderabad were working for an unlimited defensive alliance with the Company, and their leader, Mir Alam, was pledged if such a treaty were effected, to "procure the dismissal of every Frenchman in His Highness's country[1]." On the English side it was thought that "it would be a wise policy for us to check the rapid declension of the Nizam's weight among the powers of Hindosthan," as the new Governor-General (Lord Mornington) wrote to the Board of Control in 1798. And a more intimate relationship with the British was willingly accepted by the native Government as a protection against the Marathas, even with some loss of political independence. By a treaty of September, 1798, the Governor-General consented through Mir Alam, the Minister for English affairs (a significant title), to treble the subsidiary force on the disbandment of the French corps, but forbade in a despatch to the Resident, defining the course of negotiations, any acceptance, not merely invitation, of territorial cession for the maintenance of the troops, declaring that to be "an irregular ambition utterly repugnant to the disposition of this Government."

The clause quoted should in fairness be remembered for later consideration. And, in passing, there should be noticed that by the Nizam's request the enlarged force was put under the command of a British officer of high rank. It marks the beginning of the military domination. The degree of

[1] *Our Faithful Ally, the Nizam* (Fraser), p. 206, and foll.

independence resigned can be seen in the provision that foreign complications generally, and in particular with Puna, should be settled by arbitration, for since the treaty of Seringapatam two of the three allies, the Nizam and the Peshwa, had by their mutual hostilities deprived the Company of the benefit that might be expected from a triple alliance and the balance of power obtained. Further, in the event of war with Tipu under the treaty of Puna, the Nizam's French mercenaries were prepared to desert and destroying the native dynasty to fly the French standard over Hyderabad. These reflexions caused the assent of the Governor-General to be given the more readily to the long-desired treaty (Sept. 1, 1798). The subsidiary force was immediately augmented and Raymond's corps of 14,000 men disbanded by the armed diplomacy of Lord Wellesley (Mornington)[1]. It left the Nizam's dominions a protected State situated between Maratha possessions and territories over which the Company held virtual or in part actual sovereignty[2]; but as yet no suzerainty was claimed for the Company; only by the eighth article of the treaty of 1798 the point was gained for ever, that no European should be employed or retained in the Nizam's service without the knowledge and consent of the Company. In a passage[3] too long for quotation M. Chailley-Bert well remarks

[1] Raymond had died but Perron was in command and the old name was kept.

[2] Tupper, *Our Indian Protect.*, p. 20.

[3] *Les protectorats de l'Inde Brit. Annales des Sciences Politiques*, 1899, pp. 134–6, 182.

that a frontier protectorate thus became an internal one, "un protectorat de sécurité un protectorat de domination" by the law of British expansion, and was next to become "un protectorat de contrôle." Although no suzerainty was claimed by the Company some independence was certainly resigned by the Nizam, whose nominal cooperation was by such means secured in the final war with Mysore. The close of that war, on the fall of Seringapatam in 1799, saw the Nizam's dominions widely extended, but it was on terms of more marked dependence, by the partitive agreement that was incorporated in the treaty of 1800. Two years later the terms were more permanently settled, but there was no substantial change from the position assumed in 1800, when perhaps the most important compact in the State's history was signed. It sealed a perpetual and general defensive alliance between the Nizam and the Company who had "in fact become one and the same." This statement in the preamble, repeated in the articles, may be said if the phrase be allowed to express a compulsory self-subordinating equality on the Nizam's part, that only needed analysing to shew virtual dependence. His Highness resigned the right of holding direct diplomatic or belligerent relations with any power independently of the Company, in whose adjustment of all differences he was to acquiesce in consideration of the Company's protection from all unprovoked hostility or aggression, and of their station in perpetuity within his territories of an efficient subsidiary force[1]. For

[1] The treaty speaks of "The *permanent* subsidiary force."

the maintenance of this force there were ceded permanently and in full sovereignty turbulent districts presented to His Highness by the partitive treaties exacted from Mysore in 1792 and 1799, and as these territories were acquisitions from Tipu presented to the Nizam gratuitously by the Company, he lost neither money nor any portion of his original dominions, yet secured for ever the integrity of his State and the maintenance of his line[1]. There was in the bargain no departure from Lord Wellesley's former prohibition of territorial cession to which attention was drawn in anticipation of this action: there was implied no complete and sinister change in the Governor-General's opinion of the morality of territorial securities. But in another aspect a significant change of policy is clearly observed. With the fall of Tipu, the motive and means for a restoration of the balance of power in the Dekhan disappeared. The inevitable struggle that had to come with the Marathas demanded that the former theory should be replaced by the policy of British supremacy. In the light of this silent but deliberate purpose, the history from this point must be read, but the sovereignty of the Nizam was not suspended

[1] "The Deccan districts ceded by the Nizam of Hyderabad at the end of the 3rd Mysore War in 1800...are for the most part unfertile and are seldom irrigable; the rainfall is nowhere more than 30 inches, and sometimes is less than 25 inches, and the people are almost entirely dependent on land......The people are on the whole backward, and education does not flourish." Page 4 of the *Fourth Decennial Report on Progress and Condition of India*, 1901—1902. If this is the case after a century of British care the value of the territories in 1800 could have been little.

under the form of protectorate nor did his dominions form with those of the Company a unity politically, in the Indian use of the word.

Three years later the Nizam died. As a summary criticism of his reign, it may be stated that in the thirteen years preceding his accession, three reigning princes and one claimant died violent deaths, yet his "imbecile and extravagant" reign brought more disasters to his country. In every war from 1748 to 1790 (with the one exception of the Maratha campaign of 1761) the Hyderabadi Government was thwarted, with consequent loss of territory or revenue[1], nor is it possible to avoid seeing that the Nizam's alliances with the English, whether or not the superior benefit was generally, in the end, the Company's, were all that prevented the Company's ultimate advantage from being secured at the expense of, instead of in participation with, His Highness. It was only his subservience to the British that preserved the dominions from annihilation in a geographical, as well as political union of the Marathas, and his own person from being sacrificed to the ambitions of his sons.

Under these circumstances neither the prince nor his country paid an unduly heavy salvage. Indeed, as Marshman points out, Hyderabad has been remarkably and undeservedly fortunate in its history.

Nizam Ali was succeeded by his eldest son, Sikandar Jah. Some years before the Nizam's death, His Highness had made it known that he

[1] Cf. Letter (Nov. 24, 1819) from Resident to Governor-General and Lord Hastings.

purposed to apportion his realm among his three elder sons. To this project he contemplated seeking the sanction of the Marathas and the British. The Imperial sanction it is significant was not considered. But during the Nizam's severe, it was feared mortal, illness in 1797, the eldest son was appointed regent after violent opposition from the Mughalai party. Two years later the Nizam's death seemed so imminent that the Governor-General supplied the Resident with a statement (dated Nov. 6, 1799) of certain conditions, on the acceptance of which by Sikandar Jah, the British influence would be pledged to support his claim to the Nizamat. They were accepted, and every preparation made for his immediate succession when the moment should come[1]; but the Nizam's recovery caused the negotiations to be abandoned.

These conditions were included later, on the Nizam's recovery, in the treaty of 1800, and having been already discussed need only be mentioned here to indicate the position of a protected prince which Sikandar Jah would have willingly assumed, even in the absence of the famous treaty. On his ultimate accession the Nizam readily assumed that position, but it was a further anomaly that His Highness should seek, although the union of the State with the Company's Government had been fully cemented, confirmation in his office from the titular Emperor of Delhi. His father had been willing to dispense with it, but the right of confirmation was a prerogative always exercised by the over-lords of the

[1] Wellington's *Despatches*, May 19, 1803.

Nizams, whether they were the Delhi Emperors, the Company as trustees for the British Crown, or the British sovereigns. Yet it is important to assert that it is not as successors of a pageant dynasty at Delhi that the British Government claim any suzerainty over the sovereign States, as one might, for example, infer from Lord Dalhousie's subsequent reference to the Crown as the *successors* of the Delhi Emperors[1].

The dependency has been effected rather by a shifting policy of gradual and unforeseen aggression as the weakness and the strength of the contracting parties have been shewn. Consequently, while the sovereignty of the Nizams is to be freely admitted, it has a limited significance that was imposed on Sikandar Jah by his signature to a treaty of 1803, confirming all his predecessor's grants and obligations.

In the year of his accession the Maratha wars broke out again. Internecine struggles and a series of calamities had driven the refugee Peshwa to conclude with the British the treaty of Bassein, and by it to purchase forcible restitution to his power. He had entered into the same dependent relation as the Nizam had done, and so verified the conjecture and hope expressed in the 18th Article of the treaty of Hyderabad in 1800, that the head of the Marathas, as the embodiment of Hindu aspirations, might ultimately follow the action of the chief Muhammadan ruler. It depicts Hyderabad as the field of political experiments and the centre of the Company's

[1] Cf. also Westlake, *International Law*, p. 200.

problems in the matter of the native States; an aspect very illuminative throughout the States' history. Both on national and on religious grounds, Sindhia and the Raja of Nagpur were by no means prepared to acquiesce in such a situation. Nor is that less than could be expected when the contemporary feeling, expressed a little later by the Resident at Hyderabad[1], was that, "An alliance with us upon the subsidiary system, however it may contribute to the advancement of our own power, leads inevitably to the ultimate destruction of the State which embraces it." To avoid that position the Maratha confederates (who, claiming the Chauth, arrogated political supremacy over all India) marched on Hyderabad as the local representative of the subsidiary policy. The treaty of Deogaum, which concluded the subsequent British victories, released the Nizam from all tribute and obligations to the Marathas, who further ceded to His Highness, through the Company, the whole of Berar west of the river Wardha. To this he had no justifiable claim, for the Marquess Wellesley had at the beginning of the war serious occasion to weigh the advantages of declaring the Nizam a public enemy for his disloyal inclination to the Marathas, whose interest pervaded all branches of the administration[2]. But the generous policy prevailed, and the close of the war, which made the Emperor of Delhi a pensioner of the Company, put the British power in "a commanding

[1] Letter from H. Russel to Court of Directors, East India Company, 1824.

[2] Wellington's *Despatches*, Jan. 9, 1804.

position with regard to other States[1]," and made irrevocable the Nizam's decision to lean upon the British. At the same time, their assumption of responsibility for the integrity of the Nizam's dominions necessitated the formation of the Hyderabad Contingent. The subject has been frequently discussed with improper recriminations. Had His Highness acted on the reiterated advice of his chief military authority, Colonel Wellesley, repeatedly given him during the years 1803, 1804, and 1805, and maintained the levies on his personal initiative, the situation would not have involved Berar in a delicate complication which has only recently been satisfactorily arranged. And, as its consideration is demanded for a correct understanding of the Nizam's position under the Emperor of India, it will be unfolded at some length in the continuation of the narrative.

The treaty of 1800 (Article XII.) placed at the Company's immediate demand a stipulated force of His Highness's troops; but exclusive both of this, which had necessarily to be a standing army, and of the protective Subsidiary Troops provided by the Company for the Nizam, a general mobilisation of the native army at need was contemplated. It is obvious, accordingly, that the treaty contemplated two standing armies, the Contingent (as by anticipation it may be called) and the Subsidiary Force, independent of the disbanded native soldiery. But after the first Maratha war, in which the Nizam's troops had been inadequate and inefficient, or practically

[1] Wellington's *Despatches*, July 13, 1804.

non-existent, the Prince refused to support a contingent force, although threatened with the prospect of annexation or an abrogation of the alliance[1]. There was no great desire on the Company's part to maintain such alliances in which interests and ambitions clashed. At the same moment a similar connexion had been broken off with Jaipur for non-compliance with the terms of agreements made. That course with Hyderabad meant annexation; both parties knew it, and the Nizam seems to have traded upon the unwillingness of the Company to annex. All that could be effected was to have some of the State's troops organized by British officers. After the mutiny of the regular soldiery in 1813 the system was extended, a corps formed in the capital under the Resident's patronage, and named the Russel Brigade in his honour. Being paid directly from the Resident's treasury, which diverted for that purpose some of the *peshcush* due for the Northern Sarkars, it came in time to consider itself part of the Company's armies. It was one of the circumstances that made Hyderabad scarcely differ from a British province, by consolidating all powers and resources in the hands of a minister who was a British agent. Such an incident could not have occurred had not the British Indian Government been exercising through the Resident a virtual domination contrary to the instructions of the Company's Directors and, avowedly, in violation of the fundamental treaty of 1800. But it was a concession to the extremities and importunities of the Hyderabad Government, and not

[1] Wellington's *Despatches*, Jan. 19, 1805.

less legal because it did not wait for legal mechanism, at a time when the Governor-General could write, "The Nizam's territories are one complete chaos, from the Godavari to Hyderabad"; of which statement there is ample corroboration in Wellington's Despatches. The moral responsibility of the Company for sound rule was sufficient justification. The interference of the Resident was felt especially in the appointment of the native Ministers. A request for advice in their selection put forward at first spontaneously and as a little piece of flattering courtesy, became in succeeding appointments an indispensable obligation, and is one of the little connexions that have become fast bonds.

Of the native officials, the dominant Minister Chandu Lal cultivated the British friendship and received high praise from Lord Ellenborough, whose perspicacity is to be doubted. The Minister advocated as the only political remedy, "the placing of the administration of the country under the control of the British," and although this extreme step could not be taken, probably was never intended to be taken, the country's welfare justified the conversion of the Nizam into a faithful and efficient ally, by rigorous insistence on the execution of his obligations. The liability of His Highness to furnish a supplementary force in war necessitated its preparation during peace, and insomuch as it was a fixed and permanent obligation, the funds for its maintenance should have been of the same nature. So far back as 1805 Colonel Wellesley (Lord Wellington) had, with an interesting premonition of the future, proposed that the revenues of Berar should be sequestered for the cost of such a force. His advice had not been taken and the Contingent is seen to have been paid most irregularly on the sole responsibility of a subordinate minister, and, in part, by loans from local usurers. As will be patent, it was not the cost of the Contingent, but the irregularities of its payment and the whole financial confusion that made the country insolvent[1], until in 1823 the *peshcush,* due annually from the Northern Sarkars, was redeemed by the Company and the payment of the force thus left in full to the Nizam. But "the mismanagement consequent on security from internal revolt increased the burden of subsidy, and the maladministration, that partly originated the protective system, continued it."

[1] The degeneration of the State that in later times was attributed to the cost of the Contingent existed long before the creation of that force. See p. 12 of the Letter to the Court of Directors of the E. I. Co. by H. Russel, 1824.

CHAPTER III.

THE HYDERABAD ASSIGNED DISTRICTS AND THE AGITATION FOR THEIR RENDITION. SALAR JANG.

WITH Lord Wellesley's retirement had come a timid repudiation of his audacious but provident policies, and the course of non-intervention declared only a year after his departure was followed by Lord Cornwallis, Sir George Barlow, and in a less degree Lord Minto. But when Sir Charles Metcalfe became Resident at Hyderabad local reforms were pressing in their need. For the just assessment and collection of the revenue together with the settlement of the land question, the Resident introduced British supervisory officials to travel and check the local administration. He obtained for his project the sanction, cordial or not, of the Native and the Supreme Governments, although so open a suppression of His Highness' authority had not the full approval of the Governor-General, Lord Hastings. Yet these reforms were little to put against the financial depression. In Hyderabad the long established firm of William Palmer and Company were lending the Nizam's Government sums amounting to £300,000 annually for no warrantable purpose, and on no other apparent security than the prospect of territorial cession, while the private interests of the Resident, the patronage of the unsuspecting Governor-General, and the special[1] consent of the British Government, were a moral guarantee to the bankers for a rapidly increasing debt on which interest of 25 per cent. was exacted. Even in a country of high interest that can justly be called exorbitant, for it was double the highest legal rate permitted in British India and the rate on which the firm itself was borrowing. The bankers had practically usurped the government, and had become in the Dekhan a power greater than the Nizam, the East India Company or the Governor-General. Their example was followed by native usurers, one of whom, Puran Mal, between 1827 and 1829, held most of Berar in farm, and had to be expelled by the insistence of the Resident as the firm of Palmer before him. At this crisis Sir Charles Metcalfe, by counteracting the virtual minister, Chandu Lal, "saved" (to use Salar Jang's words) "the sinking State." But the whole economy of the State made the withdrawal of British domination, in view of the moral responsibility assumed, an impossibility when Nasir-ud-Daula succeeded his father and was officially proclaimed by the British in 1829. Two points are noticeable on the occasion:—it is, in the first place, significant of the gradually changing relationship, that advantage was taken of his accession to denote in the terms and courtesies of official communications

[1] Required by the Act, George III. 37, chapter 97, § 28.

the equality of the Governor-General with the Nizam; secondly, that His Highness received the British congratulations on "assuming the Sovereignty," for to no other feudatory prince is the term of sovereignty accorded by the Supreme Government.

In the internal administration of his dominions the Nizam immediately claimed and was granted absolute and unsupervised rule, with the abolition of Metcalfe's civil service, for which was substituted the farce of Native Commissions. Yet the dominant Minister, Chandu Lal, never ceased to apply for that advice and influence which could not on the now stricter observance of non-intervention be given, and the inevitable misrule ending in a protest from the Supreme Government that "they could no longer remain indifferent spectators to the disorder and misrule which had so long prevailed," a policy was sketched (but held in suspense) such as should reduce the Nizam to the position of a cypher under the advice and control of the Resident[1]. But it was merged in the fuller reconstitution shortly effected, and by no means summarily imposed. It was no longer possible to trust the good faith or the capacity of the Native Government. The religious outbreak of the Wahabis (whom Reclus calls "l'avant-garde des mahométans Sunnites") implicated the reigning family, and made it necessary in the interests of the subjects that the Nizam should remain one "whose capital is overawed by a British cantonment, and to

[1] Cf. *Despatch* of 1838.

whom a British Resident gives, under the name of advice, commands which are not to be disputed[1]."

A private letter from Hyderabad[2] almost contemporary with this sentence speaks of distress and misery and moral degradation everywhere, of labour repaid only with extortion and plunder, of deserted villages and mouldering forts.

These conditions made the cost of the Hyderabad Contingent, as it was now officially styled, a perpetual vexation to the Nizam, and equally so, as having no commercial value, to the Directors of the Company. In 1842 the Resident wrote inexactly, that the Contingent was provided for by no existing treaty. Lord Dalhousie, also[3], admitted that its maintenance in its present form was legally requisite neither by the spirit nor the letter of the treaty of 1800. The form was avowedly in Metcalfe's phrase "a joint concern between Rajah Chandu Loll and us." Yet its efficient maintenance in some form was required by treaties, and its retention in one particular form by the Nizam from 1816 gave that form a degree of official sanction that could not be immediately sacrificed to a casuistical point of equity if the undefined dependence upon the Company, assuring the Native State against foes within and without, was to continue without disadvantage to the Company or menace to His Highness.

It remained for the Company to insist upon the up-keep of the military strength while providing

Macaulay, *Clive*, Jan. 1840.

[2] *Letters of Lieut. St John*, p. 74, Feb. 1844.

[3] Minute of March 30, 1853.

that in the insolvency of the Nizam's Government from 1843 onwards the non-payment of the troops should not precipitate a military crisis and deprive the Company of any benefit from their alliance. This real apprehension was brought to the consideration of the Nizam by Lord Dalhousie in a letter which for its plain truthfulness has been censured as "full of unworthy invective and sarcasm[1]."

But though it became necessary to advance the Nizam's Government heavy sums of money, the Company, as Lord Dalhousie observed, did not become their creditor to serve any purpose of their own, nor was it other than an unwelcome extremity that His Highness had to be informed in 1843 that territorial security, the only available guarantee, would be demanded for further assistance. On December 31, 1850, which had been determined as the ultimate limit of the period in which unsecured credit could be given, the increasing debt remained unpaid, and the Resident was instructed to select districts suitable for the purpose of being temporarily ceded as the desired security. In his choice the Resident was to pay attention to their fitness for permanent retention if future contingencies should make inevitable a course in other respects undesirable. But Lord Dalhousie, whose name unfortunately is always connected with the policy of annexation, had to oppose and censure the insistence of the Resident, that for a definite number of years the whole of the Nizam's country should be ceded to the sole and exclusive management and authority of

[1] *Quarterly Review*, vol. civ., p. 265.

the Company[1]. He reminded the Resident that "we acknowledge the Nizam as an independent prince," and that were it not for the existence of the Subsidiary and Contingent Forces our relations with the State of Hyderabad would be merely those which usually are formed between two independent Powers. Nothing could be more clear than that Lord Dalhousie had no sinister contemplations of deposition and annexation such as have been ascribed to him[2]; but to the words of the sentence quoted above we must take serious exception. Lord Dalhousie was writing in some heat and with resentment of the veiled dictation of the Resident. Nor was he a lawyer to make nice distinctions in popular synonyms. A more legal mind perhaps would have discriminated between the terms sovereignty and independence[3]. His error however was not a palpable blunder, but can frequently be found in contemporary legal writers of recognized authority, and it is notorious that in the past the Indian Government has "exposed itself to misconstruction by admitting or denying the independence of particular States when in fact it meant to speak of their sovereignty[4]." With this caution the narrative can be continued. For the moment the seizure of territory was averted by the action and promises of the Nizam, but the payment being never

[1] Cf. *Despatches* of 1851.

[2] *e.g.* Briggs, *The Nizam*, i. 347.

[3] See Lee-Warner, *Protected Princes of India*, Chap. xiii.

[4] Sir H. Maine, quoted in Tupper, *Our Indian Protectorate*, page 18.

completed it became right to delay no longer in exacting the territorial security which was now taken for the liquidation of the debt and to ensure the payment of the force required by treaty to be maintained. By the people the cession was welcomed in a practical manner. There was perceptible an immediate return of the emigrants who had for more than thirty years been moving eastwards from the tracts of Berar west of the river Wardha into Nagpur, to escape the intolerable misrule that, they felt, would be corrected under the British administration.

Of the three districts selected, Berar, Dharases, and the Raichur Doab, only the first is of importance. The question of its rendition intruded into party politics in England, and has been one of the difficulties of Indian administration. Berar had been nominally in the Nizam's possession since 1724. Even in the period of the Dual Government his titular authority had been admitted by the Marathas although the dimensions of the province were repeatedly curtailed by grants to Puna or Nagpur. The Bhonsla family, inaccurately styled the Rajas of Berar, were only hereditary military collectors of the Maratha dues, levied on monies paid into the Nizam's treasury, amounting with irregular blackmail to more than half the total revenue and deriving their legality from assignments made in the time of Sivaji and Aurangzeb. In 1734 Raghoji Bhonsla obtained from the Peshwa at Puna a patent for the collection of Maratha taxes throughout Berar, then including Nagpur[1], and the Nizam's authority re-

[1] Cf. *Calcutta Review*, vol. 100.

mained more nominal than real, until after Assaye the treaty of 1804 gave nearly all Berar, including the districts east of the Wardha river, back to the Nizam's sole authority. In 1822 the latter territories were exchanged for districts west of that river, while the payment of Chauth was remitted. Yet for many years Berar was the rendezvous of the lawless. It had been torn by a Hindu revolution in 1849, and the cession of its administration, but not its sovereignty, to the British Government in 1853 was to the advantage of the Nizam's Government and treasury. Berar has dwindled with every political change, and it is not now the Berar of the early Nizams, far less the Imperial subah of that name. Indeed, of the thirteen Sarkars named in the Ain-i-Akbari, exclusive of Deogarh, which was subsequently annexed, little more than five, comprised in the Payanghat and Balaghat divisions, form the Hyderabad Assigned Districts of to-day. Nor were these ever assigned or ceded in perpetuity; that stipulation can nowhere be proved by documentary evidence, for there is a patent inaccuracy in Lord Dalhousie's farewell minute in the clause that "His Highness the Nizam had assigned in perpetual government to the Honourable East India Company the province of Berar."

The cession was to be in trust for so long a time as there remained the requirement of a contingent force. His Highness was at perfect liberty to cease to maintain the Contingent in the form employed, or gradually to disband it, provided that he were prepared for a rearrangement of treaty obligations. Of this he was informed by Lord Dalhousie and the Resident. The latter reports his answer, which apparently escaped the notice of pamphleteers:—"No: No: I do not wish to disband the Contingent......I was not speaking seriously[1]."

In view of this confession it cannot be justly said that the Contingent force was imposed upon the State for British convenience[2] if it is implied that the inconvenience of the Nizam was necessarily entailed. The position therefore is that in 1853 a new treaty was drawn up to disembarrass the Nizam and the Company, and to prevent "differences and dissensions." By it the Contingent ceased to be a part of the Nizam's army and became an auxiliary corps[3] of much the same nature as the subsidiary force, being paid out of the Nizam's revenues and at his limited disposal, while the obligation of protecting the Dominions was acknowledged again by the Company, who released His Highness from the former unlimited liability of military cooperation in time of war. This was the condition of affairs when Salar Jang succeeded his uncle in the almost hereditary office of Diwan or Chief Minister, and began an unprecedented series of reforms in which he was interrupted by the Mutiny. The defection of the chief Muhammadan ruler would have fired the South. The Governor of Bombay telegraphed to

[1] Despatch of Col. Low to the Government of India, May 1853.

[2] *Quarterly Review*, vol. 104, p. 272, "a contingent army forced for our convenience upon the State."

[3] Its strength was fixed originally at 500 infantry, 2000 cavalry and 3 field batteries.

the Resident, "If the Nizam goes, all is lost." But in his attitude of loyalty the Nizam was led by Salar Jang. Unfortunately at this moment (May 1857) His Highness died and was succeeded by his son Afzal. It cannot be told here how in the face of every incentive to join the mutineers, in resistance to many urgent influences national and religious, Salar Jang decided actively and irrevocably for the British cause,and ratified his decision with military assistance.

The suppression of the Mutiny changed the political relations of the Native States. Their nominal subjection to the Emperor which had become a virtual subordination to the East India Company was removed, on the supersesssion of the Company in 1858, by the British Crown resuming the trust it had given. At the same time the great principle of the autonomy of the Feudal States was laid down by Lord Canning. Especial honours were paid to the Nizam, and a more practical return was made in the reshaping of the old treaties between His Highness and the Company, in the course of which the district of Dharaseo and the Raichur Doab were restored. To these were added the cession of the petty State of Shorapur, which had lapsed on the rebellion and suicide of his vassal, the Raja, during the Mutiny, and the quittance of a debt of 50 lakhs of rupees. The generosity of the latter action is not quite evident in view of Lord Canning's acceptance of the fact that an almost equivalent sum was due to the Nizam through excessive expenditure on Berar. Even in the restoration of the districts of Dharaseo and the

Raichur Doab, the criticism could be made that if their retention was so apparently not a financial necessity there was no course open but to return them, unless the British Indian Government were prepared to cultivate His Highness' territories and pay, as they were bound, their profits as a gift into his treasury: and this was not a course likely to recommend itself to a commercial people. The gracefulness and generosity of the action lay in the fact that His Highness was assured in the most practical manner of the British intention to preserve for him his dominions intact and unannexed, and also that in the voluntary resignation of strategic positions (for with that definite thought they had been selected) there was a delicate avowal of confidence in the Nizam's loyalty. Had there been the same confidence in the abilities of his ministers and their power to maintain sound rule it is probable that Berar as well would have been restored[1]. On the contrary, although the debt was extinguished it was still necessary to retain Berar in trust for the purposes specified at its seizure, for the due performance of which the finances of the province now under wise administration were adequate, and the Supreme Government refused in conferring a benefit to forfeit their dignity by being bound to supply the Nizam with annual accounts of their administration of Berar.

[1] The weakness of the authorities is well shewn in an extract from the *Illustrated London News*, 26 March 1859. Although in itself of little importance it is typical:

"In fact the Rohilla war is at an end......The Rohillas cowed as they are will only give trouble in future to the Nizam's Government whose authority they systematically set at nought."

Against excessive expenditure on that purpose His Highness had other remedies and acquiesced at once in the amended plan which suggested that the surplus revenues, when the cost of the Contingent had been deducted, should be paid to him annually as the sole satisfaction. Owing to the famine no surplus could be paid for the year 1900–1901, but since the arrangement in 1853 until the recent conversion of the annual payment, thirty-six million rupees have been so remitted to His Highness. This is the more creditable in view of the ridicule once expressed at the thought that "a farthing of surplus" would ever find its way into the Nizam's treasury[1].

No further changes of importance have taken place in the State's position, except the recent settlement of Berar. Rectification of the frontiers has however been made, and questions legal and commercial have arisen, but their arrangement has invariably tended to strengthen the tie between the Nizams and the British Crown. But before an atmosphere could be created in which these questions might be discussed, the matter of the British suzerainty had to be definitely settled. Salar Jang's efforts to assert independence caused the crisis, which does not now appear to have been other than opportune. On the death of the Nizam in 1869, Salar Jang was created co-regent to act during the minority of Mir Mahbub Ali Khan who in his

[1] See an article in the *Quarterly Review*, vol. 104. Whereas in fact during the 40 years 1860—1900 the average of the annual surpluses was little less than £60,000. Indeed in one year 1887–1888 the surplus paid was £131,500.

infancy was placed on the masnad by the Resident. Of the actions of Salar Jang this is no occasion of speaking in detail. It can only be said that in discharging his office "with unwearying assiduity and an efficiency unprecedented in the Deccan[1]" he had for thirty years the sympathetic support of the Supreme Government in his internal administration.

To his early foreign policy there is the gravest objection. It became his ambition to demonstrate the independence of the State. Alleging a right to the use of International Law, he aimed at tacitly disclaiming any suzerainty of the British Crown, and fostered a passionate desire for the restoration of Berar which had been ceded to the Company on a revertible tenure by his uncle when Minister. Perhaps the word "ceded" should not be used, as Salar Jang criticised the term when employed by Lord Dalhousie and insisted that no cession but an assignment had been made. His object was expressed in a letter to Lord Northbrook[2]:—

"Either I must recover Berar, or I must be convinced of the justice of the reasons for withholding it, or—I must die."

This ambition led him to questionable actions, such as the organization of the "Reformed Troops" on the model, and to be the substitute, of the Contingent, so (as he hoped) to destroy the *raison d'être* of the British possession of Berar. Old memories of Raymond's Corps were not very tactfully revived, and in spirit at least a violation of the

1 Sir R. Temple, *Men and Events of my time in India*, p. 288.

2 Thornton, *Sir R. Meade*, p. 300.

treaty of 1853 was constituted as well as a menace given to a Protecting Power and an unjustifiable charge laid on the impoverished treasury. By other acts the lawfulness of the suzerainty exercised by the British Government was questioned. His reluctance to meet the Prince of Wales in 1875, the Railway Loan of 1876, the detected manufacture of arms, the declaration that in the matter of the vacant co-regency he determined to have no colleague, were significant of the position he was adopting. His sanction was given to many secret attempts to circumvent the Indian Government by employing the influence of the Press and the solicitations of influential private persons and high officials. On these and other grounds Lord Lytton did not hesitate to declare that the Minister's intrigues were the greatest danger in his viceroyalty, and were more grave than even war or famine[1]. In pursuance of his aims Salar Jang visited Europe in 1876, ostensibly for pleasure but in reality to press for the rendition of Berar and the disbandment of the Contingent. His note which was virtually an attack on the whole of the Government's action towards Hyderabad was fairly considered by Lord Northbrook and the home Government. The Secretary for India, Lord Salisbury, tactfully but with firmness refused to alter the political situation during the Prince's minority, or in any way to discuss the validity of the treaties of 1853 and 1860.

But before proceeding to England the Minister directed a propaganda through the English Press.

[1] Letter quoted in Thornton's *Sir R. Meade*.

An attempt was made to procure the adoption of the question into party politics as the matter of the Karnatik had been. Pamphleteering was adroitly employed, but the sheets issued contained no arguments that the most superficial study of documents could not shew to be based on historical inaccuracies and perversions. They imputed motives that could be categorically refuted by reference to the Governor-General's Minute (dated May 27, 1851) upon the occasion of the cession, and they were in tone most discourteous[1]. Consistency was not a matter of great moment, and, while advocating generosity in return for loyalty, they did not shrink from disparaging that same fidelity as unpatriotic, in the alliterative sneer that "Patriotism is not a popular virtue among pensioned and protected potentates[2]."

In 1877 the Minister was advised that his attendance at the great Imperial Darbar could not be permitted unless the suzerainty of the Queen-Empress was unquestioned, for he had at that moment presented a second and more proper memorial on the Berar question. By his attendance he gave evidence how cognisant he was that the suzerainty was necessary and inevitable. Soon afterwards he formally announced the full acceptance of

[1] *e.g.* "The Case on Behalf of His Highness the Nizam in the matter of the Berar Provinces," 1875.

[2] See *Quarterly Review*, vol. 104, p. 259, and the references to a "Garbled Blue Book" (note on p. 266) and to the "Assigned Districts filched by a series of manœuvres" (p. 266). Of course Salar Jang must not be held responsible for the language of his supporters.

Lord Salisbury's decision in the matter of his appeal. The Viceroy had in a private letter to the Resident expressed the opinion that in any negotiations former treaties and the whole military position would have to be considered, on the understanding that the British Government alone should protect the Nizam's dominions and that His Highness retain only a small body of troops for the maintenance of his dignity. In consequence it was admitted by Salar Jang, that seeing the reopening of the question meant a general revision of existing treaties he could not advise it, for "regarding as he did the old Treaties as the most precious gems in the Nizam's possession, he would not on any account have them touched or revised[1]."

His subsequent actions were declared by the Governor-General in Council to be those of an "enlightened and experienced friend to the British Government." His mistake had lain in the fact that he was of those "qui ont pris les souvenirs pour les espérances[2]," as it has been, rather pathetically, expressed.

The wisdom of retaining a security in the Assigned Districts was apparent three years after Salar Jang's death. Even in his lifetime Hyderabad had been styled the Constantinople of the East. But now travellers found dissension, intrigue, cabals everywhere, and little interest taken in public affairs[3].

[1] Given in Thornton's *Memoir of Meade*, p. 334.

[2] Quoted from Thornton, *ibid*.

[3] "There are many private cabals and dissensions among the nobles as well as among the relatives of the Nizam, and little

It was a period of retrogression with great public scandals and incompetent administration. Native opinion was resentful that at this stage the "mischievous meddlesomeness of the Residency" was most active and dominant. But it is an axiom, that the extent of intervention is in inverse proportion to that of sound rule, and we are not surprised to find calumnies to the effect that the internal ruin of the State and the debauchment of its Prince were maliciously directed by a sinister Foreign Office, whose policy of organized aggression was intended to produce annexation[1]. The foreign relations of the State were, in sharp distinction, irreproachable. The same year in which these assertions were made, His Highness offered loyal co-operation in Egypt and in Afghanistan: but most of all in 1887, he surprised India and Europe with the offer of £600,000 and men towards the defence of the North Western frontier. To this he added an expression of his willingness to take the field in person if occasion arose.

This splendid example (if more unselfish than the State's finances warranted) was an action unparalleled, as occurring in a time of peace and as an acknowledgement of some responsibility for the expenses of the Central Government. The money could not be accepted but the offer presented critical features. It committed His Highness and his successors to a perpetual fidelity, and evoked similar advances from

interest is taken in the administration of public affairs." *Last Voyage of Lady Brassey*.

[1] Cf. W. S. Blunt, *Ideas about India*, p. 121, 1885.

other native princes, but it also shewed a quick grasp of political opportunity and gave a decided diplomatic advantage to His Highness, by forestalling the inevitable disarming of his forces on any invasion of the North Western frontier in the absence of such an offer[1]. With still wider consequences, it necessitated the consideration whether the Native States should enter on a military career trusted rather than supervised, and happily the more generous policy prevailed.

With this career speculations as to the future will be concerned, but as an introduction to anticipations of the direction in which future development may be expected, it is desirable to state in brief, as a corollary to the narrative of the Hyderabad State and its origin, a summary of the results which have been reached, so far as they touch the Nizam's position towards the British Crown.

[1] Cotton, *New India*, p. 22, 1885.

CHAPTER IV.

THE PRESENT IN ANTICIPATION OF THE FUTURE. BERAR AND ITS RENDITION. SOME ASPECTS OF THE FUTURE.

THE British Crown claims no right over the Nizam by virtue of succession to the Emperors of Delhi, but "The imperial right over the protected States appears to present a peculiar case of conquest operating by assumption and acquiescence[1]." In respect of Hyderabad, diplomacy and circumstances effected this form of conquest, and it is impossible to fix any definite date as the time when the State was incorporated in India, in the technical sense of the term. Internationally the Dominions are not a State; both theoretically and actually they are under the effective and habitual control of a superior political power. But there is a constitutional sense in which they may be so called in that the legislation and the jurisdiction of the Supreme Government

[1] Westlake, *Chapters etc. on International Law*, p. 209. For the opposite opinion, see M. Chailley-Bert, p. 169, *op. cit.* "Héritiers des empereurs de Delhi, ils tenaient d'eux une suzeraineté d'allure féodale."

are not in force in the Dominions, although the State is subject to the King-Emperor as its executive, and to the British Parliament as its legislative, head, whose enactments are applied to the State through the British Indian Government. In other words it may be stated that Hyderabad is feudal in its political system and federal in its administration, while the general bond is imperial. We have apparently no precise term in International Law to define the situation.

In the use of such terms, which are conventional and serviceable, it must be remembered that Sir H. Maine and Sir A. Lyall agree in the caution that Indian feudalism is by no means that of Mediaeval Europe. And the extent of the suzerainty and subordination is vague; we have never had (perhaps wisely) a clear declaration of the position and the policy of the British Crown towards the Native States[1]. The former has however been well sketched in the sentence that "from a condition of subordinate isolation the allied and protected States were raised to the position of partners and were finally united to the British Government[2]."

The position attained is an intermediate one between the status of self-governing and Crown colonies, while there is enjoyed a constitutional, but not, from the point of view of international law, an independent sovereignty, and this derives no authority from any delegation. This has been called by Bryce an imperfect sovereignty, by others semi-

[1] *Madras Review*, 1898.

[2] Lee-Warner, *Protected Princes*, p. 368.

sovereignty (mi-souveraineté), and it must now be accepted in contradiction of the opinion of Austin that legal sovereignty, as distinguished from independence, is formal and may be divisible or limited[1]. And of the varying degrees of sovereign power which the Native Princes of India possess the maximum is held by His Highness the Nizam, who is in the enjoyment of the marked sovereign rights of coinage, dating from the time of the mutiny when His Highness's monies ceased to bear the inscription of the Delhi Emperors, of taxation, the infliction without appeal of capital punishment, and the bestowal of honorific titles on his own subjects. In practice the vagueness that clouds the theoretical status of His Highness disappears. As in autonomous States generally, the administration is subject to, but not controlled by, the Supreme Government, which possesses over the ruling prince powers of suspension and deposition. At Hyderabad these powers are represented by the Resident, acting as the channel of communication for the expression of the views of the Supreme Government, for Native States have not the right of exchanging embassies with the Suzerain or one another. Till the beginning of the nineteenth century an envoy from Hyderabad was commissioned to the Foreign Office at Calcutta, but the practice ceased in the Residency of Col. Kirkpatrick who first held the dual position as the intermediary of both Governments.

Representing the Governor-General in Council the Resident has jurisdiction over the military

[1] Cf. Salmond's *Jurisprudence*, Appendix II.

cantonments and the lines of communication. In councils his voice is preponderant but not predominant, and in all internal legislation and administration the Nizam is independent. British municipal law does not run in his dominions, although its énactments are respected as regulations; provincial governors have no supervision over the State, nor their courts any .jurisdiction. So far is theory carried that extradition treaties nominally exist between the two powers, seeing that to permit the introduction of British judicial systems would be tantamount to annexation. Yet practically the administration is coming to be, in the main, the same as that in the provinces, with the distinction that there are no European officials appointed by the Crown, as in Egypt, to administrative posts; for the Resident's powers are ex-territorial.

In default of that privilege the British Government possesses the right of sanction and veto over all important proceedings in the State.

Such being, very briefly sketched, the position of the Dominions it remains to see in what particulars modification may be anticipated. There was a time when before all other considerations the ultimate rendition of the Assigned Districts would have demanded discussion. That is no longer so urgent a consideration, as the matter advanced a stage when in 1902 the Viceroy visited Hyderabad and amicably settled the long-pending Berar question on terms by which the Nizam relinquished for ever all claim to a restoration of the province or to the exercise of territorial jurisdiction in the same, while retaining his nominal sovereignty over the districts[1]. This will be recognized by flying His Highness' flag by the side of the British. In lieu of the annual surplus of revenue to which he was entitled there will be paid the assured sum of £167,000 a year. This revenue will no longer be a fluctuating income, and the transaction has enabled the Hyderabad contingent with which Berar is historically associated to be reshaped. The familiar sequence is apparently working out, and if precedents afford any safe guide in anticipating the future, the ultimate restoration of Berar is not to be considered probable. The school of politicians that has advocated similar proposals will not, it is expected, be in a position to effect them until the Imperial bond has been drawn too tight and a more distant retrospect shewn the question in a better light.

It would not be surprising if the lessons of the Northern Sarkars should be taken to heart, and the present annual payment in respect of Berar capitalized at some time of financial embarrassment on the part of the Nizam's Government. One would point to the urgent need of financial supervision in the years 1896 and 1897, followed by severe famine in 1900 and 1901, and by an unusually severe attack of plague in 1903, as well as to the present tendency towards an alteration in the dimensions of the

[1] Details of the agreement are given in Parliamentary Paper Cd. 1321, 1902. The precise wording of the treaty is that "His Highness the Nizam whose sovereignty over the Assigned Districts is reaffirmed leases them to the British Government in perpetuity, etc."

presidencies, with a view to their subdivision, in the course of which Berar might well be absorbed into British India. It is true that there are not such necessitous reasons for the incorporation of Berar as there were in the case of the Sarkars, and there is the further consideration that if Berar is administered by the Chief Commissioner of the Central Provinces its inhabitants may have to resort for justice to Nagpur, the former seat of a Maratha Government, and obviously that would be unwelcome among Dekhani Muhammadans. Berar however was in fact placed under the Government of the Central Provinces in 1903, and it remains to see the force of the objection, which is not a strong one. Certainly there would be an advantage in realizing the design, with which Lord Canning and Sir Ch. Wood were credited so long ago as 1860, of uniting in one lieutenant-governorship the whole of the cotton fields of Central India by the amalgamation of Nagpur and Berar[1]. It is impossible not to see a stage of this development reached by the combination, taking place in April, 1874, of the East and West Berars (to use the common names) into one financial and administrative charge under one commissioner.

As a necessary consequence of any alteration in the tenure of the Assigned Districts, there was foreseen, by those acquainted with Hyderabad affairs, a reconsideration of the Hyderabad Contingent. Now that there were means of rapid transport such as to enable large forces to be thrown into India at

[1] See letter in the *Times* of 20 February, 1863.

short notice, it was felt that the retention of the Contingent was no longer so imperative as formerly, and that if, from the other aspect, India was considered a great military depot and training ground, the substitution of British for native troops was desirable. This opened the whole question of the military position. The native troops in British India were and are more than double the number of the British forces[1], and His Highness the Nizam maintained the largest if not the most efficient army in the Peninsula. His chiefs and nobles could number their military retainers by the thousand, and on the irregular troops, who might well be expected as in 1890 to be often uncontrollable, more than half the military expenditure of the State was lavished. The whole military strength of the Nizam was out of all proportion to the size of the Hyderabad State and the ratio existing in British India. On a lenient computation the forces were five times too numerous in the absence of any frontiers to be protected, and this army, which was considerably inferior to the native regiments of the line, drained the revenues of an overtaxed State and absorbed the payments from Berar. It was supposed to be supervised and if necessary intimidated by the Contingent, a tenth of its size.

This was the position as it appeared to those observant not more than two years ago, and much that has been written of in the past tense remains

[1] Exclusive of the Hyderabad Contingent (7454 strong) the sanctioned military establishment for 1902-3 was as follows:—British Troops 73,509, Native Troops 146,745.

still unaltered. But in one respect there has been a change of more than casual interest. The Hyderabad Contingent, of which traces run like guiding thread through the maze of the State's political history, was felt to be in itself a relic of a position long since abandoned. Its reorganization or even abolition (with the transference of its duties to an Anglo-Indian garrison drawn from Madras or Bombay) was anticipated. It was felt a less probable alternative that a national militia should be raised on the model of the action taken with Nagpur in 1829. With a population mainly Hindu and an existing military class of Muhammadans the better course is seen to have been the one recently taken on the occasion of the last Viceregal visit to Hyderabad, when the Contingent was absorbed into the Indian army and provision made for the gradual reduction of the irregular soldiery. The position certainly needed modification, and any speculations as to the future that were made in the last few years necessarily included the question of the military position. In this as well as in the matter of Berar the recent transactions enable a more intelligent forecast to be made than was possible before, as an indication has now been given of official intentions and policy.

Since the 1st of October 1902 the Hyderabad Contingent has been paid by the Government of India. At the end of the year 1902–3 the Contingent was placed under the orders of the Commander-in-Chief in India and thus became part of the regular Indian army. It then consisted of four regiments of cavalry, four batteries of artillery and six battalions of infantry, in all nearly seven thousand five hundred men. As was anticipated these forces have now been scattered. Early in the year 1903–4 the artillery was disbanded, the cavalry being then incorporated in the Bombay command and the infantry in that of Madras. During the year 1902–3 about £114,000 was paid on account of the Contingent, and it will therefore be seen that a considerable sum will now be available for other purposes.

The purposed reduction in the number of the irregular troops, following the abolition of the mercenary force, will leave free a great annual revenue for the material benefit of the people and the restitution of a sound financial position. This course of action has constantly been enjoined upon His Highness. Even so lately as 1892 the Viceroy, Lord Lansdowne, pressed, during his visit of inspection in that year, for the attentive reconsideration of the State's finances, and suggested a diminution of the irregular army. Indeed scarcely a year passes but that the annual administrative report of India contains a reiteration of these two important points. For several consecutive years since 1895 there has been a considerable excess of expenditure over income, and in the year 1901 the Nizam appointed a member of the Indian Civil Service to reform the finances and reduce expenditure. It cannot be said that the danger is yet over.

In the internal administration anything of the nature of popular control lies outside practical consideration. In some parts of British India municipal responsibilities may be with advantage and confidence entrusted to the educated population, who even feel strong enough to undertake the conduct of presidential parliaments and a degree of home rule. However that may be, such is not the situation in Hyderabad, where European education and missionary efforts (as typical of the spread of western ideals) have made in one case the slightest, in the other no, impression. The latest educational statistics, given by the census of 1901, shew that the literates are only three per cent. of the population. This proportion is much lower than should be found in the greatest and richest of Native States; it is also an average greatly below that of backward India as a whole. In the other respect, religious toleration carrying with it equality of civil rights is not yet a year old. It all points to the thought that only through the Native Princes supported by a European bureaucratic class, gradually to be replaced by native officials, can progress be made. Lord Macaulay was of opinion that India cannot have a free Government but may have the next best thing, a firm and impartial despotism[1]. Such a despot will always be found in a strong Minister or, in default, in the political Resident, but the hope of the future is placed in the possible education of an enlightened oligarchy that could make of the Nizam's dominions a compact and self-sufficient State. In one capable man there is little assurance of permanent success. That was seen with Salar Jang, and again in Kashmir where a strong and efficient native Minister such as Gulab

[1] *Life and Letters*, p. 287, ed. 1890.

Sing found a weak and poor successor, with the result that now there is practically a British administration. A ruling class of the type indicated would satisfy the popular ideal, and it cannot be forgotten that, although the doctrinaire may build up eclectic schemes of administration, even a just Government (as Mountstuart Elphinstone has written) will not be a blessing if at variance with the habits and character of the people. Another authority, with whom upon this question an agreement can seldom be reached, has in this case admirably stated that there is "no promise or hope of permanence anywhere but in the reformed native State. That and not the model British province is the mature and wholesome fruit of imperial cultivation[1]." And such a reformation should involve the permanence of the Native State radically unaltered. There is for instance in the Nizam's dominions an excellent opportunity for the politician to see the natural working out of a scheme of decentralisation in government and administration that should leave untouched general politics and imperial questions. But premature liberty would be the greatest misfortune, and for that reason some slight exception must be taken to remarks in the "Famine Notes" of His Highness the Gaikwar of Baroda. "It is, however, a pity," he writes, "that the British Government is so fond of centralisation, and so strictly compels native States to ask for its sanction in matters where they ought to be entirely free to make their own arrangements, even if necessary, in concert with other neighbouring

[1] Major Evans Bell, *Our Vassal Empire* (Preface).

native States. If native States are to be preserved in all their vitality, it is necessary to give them greater freedom and promote in them habits of self-reliance, and to stop this policy of chaperoning done out of mistaken kindness. Some blunders are preferable to imbecility and want of timely decision. The tendency of the British authorities in their treatment of native administrations in periods of famine seems at times too assertive of supremacy. This proclivity tends to create a gulf between the native governors and the governed, and all manly interest in the pursuits of good and consistent rule is discouraged[1]."

The suggestion of interstatal relations here made by the Gaikwar will be considered later in a different context; for the rest, one would agree that if the open action of the Resident could be dispensed with it would be an advantage, but the moral responsibility of the British Government for the welfare of the subjects of the Native Princes (and that is the chief imperial bond) makes one view with suspicion the thought that the education of the princes in their duties should be acquired by experiments upon their peoples. The objections to this and to the more empirical scheme that might be developed out of Major Bell's opinion just quoted, namely the multiplication of Native States by the reestablishment of annexed territories, are many, but nowhere has the matter been put more justly than in the words of Mr (afterwards Sir Richard) Jenkins, Resident of Nagpur more than half a century ago. The contrast

[1] Quoted in *The Failure of Lord Curzon* (Anon.).

will be more effective if the contemporary position of the State of Hyderabad is borne in mind. Speaking of the British intervention he remarked that "the effect of these arrangements has in every respect been beneficial, nor has there been any material innovation introduced into the native system calculated to obstruct the restoration of the native government, except the spirit in which it has been administered, a spirit of purity and justice which must be preserved if such a restoration is intended as a real benefit either of the prince or his people[1]." The great initial difficulty is to assure the maintenance of British ideals. If that could be done the prosperity of a Native State might well induce some approximation of the British Indian Provinces to its system and to the administrative decentralisation which has in various forms received the sanction of such different characters as Mr Bright[2], Mountstuart Elphinstone[3], Lord Mayo, and the Marquis of Ripon. Not only do the Native States afford an admirable field for administrative experiments, but they also react against the inevitable tendency in British India to excessive departmentalism.

These conjectures presuppose that the reigning dynasty will be maintained in something more than titular sovereignty. The attitude of the Indian Government to the Native Princes favours such a presumption and therefore many obvious anticipations can only be mentioned for rejection. Of these the annexation of the State to British India directly

[1] Quoted in *Gazetteer of Southern India*, p. 633.

[2] Speech on the budget of Sir Charles Wood, August, 1859.

[3] *Collected Papers*, p. 73.

or by lapse might be considered a possible event. It could be argued that in the action we should be displacing a ruler as foreign as ourselves in race and religion, and one whose ancestors were not much earlier in the field than our own. Detractors have said that His Highness' family is of neither very ancient nor exalted descent; that his Government have but two claims to British gratitude, in the events of the Mutiny and the famous offer of 1887, while nowhere else is the ruling caste so obtrusive, so alien, or so barren in achievements that merit the admiration of the people. This is disparagement to extenuate, rather than argument to justify, the action suggested. If it were worth while the clauses could be considered separately and different conclusions perhaps obtained; it is however better to weigh real arguments such as those contained in Lord Dalhousie's well-known minute advocating the annexation of the Punjab[1]. The statements there contained will be found no longer apposite if referred to Hyderabad. The acknowledged possession (the value of which he especially emphasized) has now actually devolved upon the British people, among whom however are included the State's own subjects, to whom the pageant of a local throne is a resident incentive and encouragement to patriotism, local perhaps in the people, but imperial in the rulers. Further, there is the treaty obligation of maintaining the Asafia house, so that to appropriate the territories by the doctrine of lapse would be a grave violation of the treaty of 1858 and of the Adoption

[1] See its outlines in Hunter's *Dalhousie* (Rulers of India) p. 81.

Sanads such as could only be warranted by most exceptional occurrences. It is true that the treaties have been, and are, considered subordinate to the supreme interests of the Empire or the State's subjects, and, though such a position was never contemplated at the first, it is now generally understood and accepted that the treaties are scarcely more than limitations of its own actions which the Imperial Government imposed under other conditions, and is pleased to maintain in preference to reshaping its compacts on paper as well as in practice. This has been laid down as a principle by the highest legal authorities[1], and is a matter of common sense that scarcely needs emphasis. It affords the answer to a recent anonymous criticism of the present Viceroy's action. Referring primarily to a Sanad dealing with Chota-Nagpur only, it is capable of a wider application. "Are ancient obligations" (says the critic quoting in full from the *Bengali* of Calcutta) "to be scattered to the winds in the presence of new conditions? To say that they may be disregarded is to lay down a most dangerous doctrine which would sap the confidence of the rulers of Native States in the British Government. The treaties with the great states of Hyderabad, Gwalior, and Baroda were concluded under circumstances which no longer exist. The condition of things has changed; and are the treaties with these great Feudatories to be disregarded on that account[2]?"

[1] Hall's *International Law*, p. 29 note.

[2] Quoted in *The Failure of Lord Curzon* (Anon. 1903) p. 78.

To this the answer must be that the treaties and contracts are undoubtedly capable of modification and revision at the will of the supreme power, even to the extent of the deprivation of the Prince's sovereignty. But in this case what is possible is not probable, and the conclusion reached is that the Native Princes are now for ever a part of Indian government, and that in particular the State of Hyderabad will be, according to the wish of the British Indian Government expressed in Hyderabad city by the late Viceroy, Lord Lansdowne, a permanent part of the Empire, provided that the subjects of His Highness the Nizam shall have through maladministration no cause to complain that their interests have been sacrificed by the non-incorporation of their country in British India. Hyderabad is no longer destined to follow the example of Oudh, and to be kept in the meantime in the circle of the Ring-Fence policy as a field for expansion in the future. The restitution of a native dynasty to Mysore after the British administration had lasted more than half a century cannot be dismissed as bearing no indication of the trend of British policy towards other native States. It is the precise meaning of the policy that is in question. There are not wanting those who see in it an indication that the British no longer believe their administrative tutelage of India lasting in its present vague and imperial form. It has been interpreted as a slow recoil right along the line. England it is said is yielding to the pressure of circumstances, and to the fatality of the

East. She anticipates the inevitable separation and accepts it[1].

But it is preferable to think that English policy, little attentive to logic, contemptuous of fine ready-made schemes (such in France is its reputation), is again letting itself be guided by experience alone and proceeding slowly with constant readjustments[2], such as will bind the Indian Empire more closely in fact if not in theory. As conservative in the retention of legal forms as the Roman Empire, the British Government will probably not weaken the tie between Hyderabad and itself by any such fiction as the substitution of an envoy for the political Resident at the native court. The proposition has been made, but it is difficult to see how the position may be so strengthened, or to believe that the unreality of the flattery would enhance the dignity of His Highness. It may however be expected that substantial freedom of action will continue to be permitted so far as is consistent with the maintenance of British paramountcy. But how to exercise a preponderating influence otherwise than by annexation is not immediately obvious. It is a difficulty which in Egypt also has presented itself for solution. Between Egypt and Hyderabad a

[1] Émile Boutmy (de l'Institut), *Annales des Sc. Politiques*, 1889, p. 545.

[2] "La politique anglaise peu soucieuse de la logique, dédaigneuse des grand plans d'ensemble construits longtemps d'avance, se laisse guider par l'expérience procédant lentement par retouches constantes." Achille Viallate, *Ann. des Sc. Pol.* 1899, p. 656. See also Despagnet, *Sur les Protectorats*, pp. 140 and 142.

parallel has been drawn and expressed for the first time (in the writer's knowledge) by Col. Malleson in 1883[1]. The original inhabitants of both countries he points out are ruled by alien Muhammadans, and the dominant class in Hyderabad is descended from the same Turki tribe as are the rulers of Egypt. Both countries have prior to our presence been occupied by the French in the days of their colonial activity, and in both cases their domination would succeed our withdrawal; further, both need for their existence some kindly foreign suzerainty which for Hyderabad from its geographical position can only be British. For this reason to withdraw entirely from Hyderabad is impossible: it would certainly mean the dislocation of the Madras Presidency and perhaps religious war. In brief, the sovereignty of Hyderabad and its existence as a State, and as the premier Native State, may be well expected to continue with ever growing amenities and facilities extended to, and reciprocated by, the Supreme Government, whose duty it will remain to energize the native rule and assist its development of administrative functions.

The question arising from this conclusion is of the position of His Highness the Nizam in the future, and here also there are lessons gained by experience of British policy to direct anticipations. The uniform tendencies of British administration have been to exalt the status of the Indian chiefs, whom in Sir William Lee-Warner's opinion it is wrong to call feudatories. Accepting the correction,

[1] *Proceedings of Roy. Col. Instit.* 10th April, 1883.

although inclining to the belief that the difference between him and Mr Tupper in this matter is merely verbal[1], we shall be right in describing the native princes as sovereigns of petty States and not in assigning them to a rural aristocracy or peerage. With a certain section of the press it has been customary to call His Highness the Nizam "a mere nobleman[2]," and this most inadequate and designedly offensive title is perhaps based upon Lord Canning's statement of policy that "we do deliberately desire to keep alive a feudal aristocracy where one exists," but this false analogy leads to the mischievous conclusion of Élisée Reclus that it is purposed to make of "ces descendants de souverains une grande aristocratie terrienne comme celle des lords anglais[3]." His Highness the Nizam is a reigning sovereign with a feudatory prince, the Raja of Gadwal, under him, and it will be to the advantage of all to maintain the local sovereignty, not only for its popularity, but also because the Indian peoples look to persons rather than to systems, and consider high birth the qualification for office, while the Supreme Government finds in the greater permanence of the official

[1] Lee-Warner, *Protected Princes of India*, and Tupper, *Our Indian Protectorate*.

[2] *The Friend of India*, 23rd April and 28th Aug. 1863.

[3] *Géographie Univ.* VIII. 706. Quoted also by Lee-Warner and others, everywhere with condemnation. In sharp contradiction see Lord Curzon's words reported in the *Times*, July 21, 1904: "I have always been a devoted believer in the continued existence of the native States in India, and an ardent well-wisher of the Native Princes, but I believe in them not as relics but as rulers, not as puppets but as living factors in the administration. I want them to share the responsibilities as well as the glories of British rule."

staff and in their tie of nationality a more adequate interpretation to the people of its workings and aims, as well as a valuable safeguard against ill-suited legislation; but the prince's activity must be confined to his own dominions. On the 1st of January, 1877, a council of the Empire was formed to obtain the advice and cooperation of the Princes and Chiefs of India. This Diet it must be admitted has never done business, nor existed at all except on paper. It has been suggested by Sir Roper Lethbridge that it should be called into being and intrusted with the discussion of broad imperial questions. It would presumably, if it was to be a responsible body, correspond in some degree to that peculiar feature of the German Empire, the Bundesrath, and form a legislative and executive council, a court of appeal, and an imperial cabinet in which the Supreme Government would exercise the extensive veto which the German Emperor as King of Prussia exercises in its pattern, the Bundesrath[1]. If all the native States stood in the same position to the Supreme Government as Hyderabad does, it might be possible, by adopting the German principle of assigning voting power in accordance with rank and importance, to form such a Diet. But this is not the case: it would be found that many dominions were, like Alsace-Lorraine, nothing more than imperial territory (in the German term, "Reichsland"), and in consequence entitled to no vote in the council, while in no sense does the British authority in India correspond to the hegemony of

[1] Cf. A. L. Lowell, *Governments and Parties in Continental Europe*, i. 258, etc.

Prussia. It also appears to be a most inexpedient plan to introduce the tie of confederation which would be created by such a body, and would be likely to alter the political situation by effecting interstatal relationships contrary to the principle of isolation, from which no departure seems advisable. Opposed to Sir Roper Lethbridge's scheme are all the chief authorities qualified to speak of the Indian States, and in whatever direction the present position may be changed it may confidently be expected that Lord Lytton's Imperial Council will not be resuscitated, but may be dismissed from the politics of Hyderabad[1].

In particular we cannot forget that the British attitude towards the Nizam will be affected by the recognition that His Highness, as head of the Muslim powers in India, has over Muhammadans an influence which can be turned to political advantage. The Muhammadan subjects of the British Empire form almost half the Muhammadan population of the world; the British Empire is the greatest Muslim power, and Hyderabad is the principal and most powerful of the twenty-two Muhammadan States in India. His Highness the Nizam is a much greater prince in revenues and the number of his subjects than the Amir of Bokhara who is termed the head of Islam in Central Asia, or the Shereef of Morocco who could probably challenge the legal right of the Sultan of Turkey to the Khalifate. Should the Sultan ever forfeit his throne or (*de facto*) Khalifate,

[1] For a discussion of the suggestion see *Asiatic Quarterly Review* (2nd series), vol. 7 (1893–4), p. 59; vol. 8, p. 36; vol. 10, pp. 312—344.

the Nizam not improbably might become the virtual head of Islam. In that position there would be no danger of religious war of Musalmans against the British Crown, certainly not of the Suni Muhammadans of Hyderabad, who are locally in the minority; and, as Hyderabad is not suited for the purposes of a religious propaganda, the influence wielded by an active creed might be more safely employed. Any *jihad* has been declared illegal according to the tenets of their faith by law doctors of Mecca, Northern India, and the Calcutta Muhammadan Society, who have all formally declared India to be a land of The Faith (Dar-ul-Islam). Yet, as Sir W. Hunter pointed out, there is a question of their action if a Muhammadan power were to attack British India. To this it could be answered that there is reason to believe that bonds of religious hatred and religious sympathy would not hold. For the first time in history, in the Boer War, the Muhammadans of Hyderabad prayed for the success of infidel arms, and in Hyderabad itself religious disabilities have, if only recently, been rescinded by its Muhammadan ruler.

In anticipating the course of future changes it is impossible to shape an elaborate and all-embracing scheme. All that can be attempted is to take some salient features of the existing régime, and to speculate upon the alterations which may justly be inferred from a knowledge of the present, and a presumed detection of political tendencies. In this historical consideration nothing else has been attempted, for nothing is easier than to spin prophecies if the date of their realization is put sufficiently remote. One other point, however, remains to be contemplated. No word is commoner to-day than Zollverein; its companion, Kriegsverein, has not been equally adopted into the statesman's vocabulary, but in 1891 the late Lord Salisbury stated that the hope of the future in India lay in the formation of such a double bond. The projected customs union may if realized affect Hyderabad considerably, for commercially more than politically will the State develop. Its climate is good, temperature equable, and though deficient in rainfall the State has a fertile soil which under irrigation produces good crops of maize, rice, mustard, fruits, indigo, wheat, oil-seeds, cotton, and tobacco. In the Singareni mine the State possesses the second largest coal supply of India. In pasturage and cattle the Dominions abound, and for horse-breeding have a name, but there is need for an extensive development of the resources. "Potentially," it has been said, "the Nizam's territory is of the richest in India......the people are well-to-do and they deserve their prosperity. Besides the crops and cattle enthusiasts believe there is enough gold in Hyderabad to cut the throat of the Klondike, and beggar the Rand[1]." Therefore in any commercial readjustments Hyderabad will be interested and Berar also. Financial disturbances in the United States in July, 1903, and in 1904, seriously threatened the cotton trade of England. Such a crisis would be obviated by the extension of cotton growing in the Empire. In India apparently, as a whole, the

[1] *In India*, G. W. Steevens.

extension is not possible, unless in Burma, but the thick black soil in the undulating valley of Berar already produces the finest cotton crop in India, and it is estimated that, with only one-half of the whole area now cultivated, half as much again could be so developed.

Of a Kriegsverein, Lord Salisbury's second proposition, there is on many sides promise, but nowhere more markedly than in the new aspirations of the protected princes to incorporate themselves more actively in the defence of the Empire. It was initiated by the Nizam's famous offer in 1887, to which attention has been already drawn in detail. On that occasion the *Times* (of 27th September, 1887) contained the pertinent comment that "in the union of those who will suffer is to be found absolute security, both now and in the future, and the Nizam has shown that this union exists."

For sixteen years there has been no necessity to depart from the estimation there given of His Highness the Nizam, and there is the happiest augury for the future (as well as a satisfactory confirmation of the past) in the recent utterance of His Highness at the Darbar of Delhi in January, 1903, when he spoke of the pleasure it had been to him to be present and "after the custom of my ancestors to show in a simple, straightforward, and soldierly manner by word and deed my historical friendship and loyalty." In the preservation of that friendship and loyalty the future of the Hyderabad State lies.

APPENDIX.

AUTHORITIES IRRESPECTIVE OF PARLIAMENTARY PAPERS.

Authors		Editions
AITCHISON	Treaties, etc. Vol. 8. Part ii.	1892
ANON.	The Nizam of Hyderabad and the Berar Provinces. Case on Behalf of His Highness, etc., in the matter of Berar. Memorandum, etc.[1]	1876
	Armies of the Native States of India.	1884
BELL (Major E.)	The Empire in India.	1864
BERNIER	Travels in the Mogul Empire.	1826
BLUNT (W. S.)	Ideas about India.	1885
	The Future of Islam.	1882
BRIGGS (H. G.)	Ferishta's Hist. (to 1612).	1829
	The Nizam.	1861
BRYCE	Studies in History and Jurisprudence.	1901
CASTONET DES FOSSES	L'Inde Française avant Dupleix.	1887
CHAILLEY-BERT	Les protectorats de l'Inde Britannique (i. and ii.). (Annales de l'école libre des Sciences Politiques.)	1899
DIGBY (W.)	India for the Indians and—for England.	1885

[1] *Brit. Museum Catalogue*, 8023 dd. 21.

Authors		Editions
Elphinstone	History of India (Vols. 1 and 2).	1841
Fraser (H.)	Our Faithful Ally, the Nizam.	1865
Gribble	History of the Deccan (Vol. 1).	1896
Guyon (Abbé)	Histoires des Indes Orient.	1744
Hamont	Dupleix d'après sa corresp. inédite.	1881
(Tibulle)	Lally-Tollendal (La fin d'un Empire, etc.)	1887
Hollingberry	A history of his late Highness, Nizam Alee Khaun (and Appendix).	1805
Hunter	Dalhousie (Rulers of India).	1890
(Sir W. W.)	The Indian Musalmans.	1871
	Imperial Gazetteer of India.	1881
Ilbert	Government of India.	1898
Kaye	Life and Corresp. of Charles, Lord Metcalfe.	1854
Keene (H. G.)	Fall of the Moghul Empire.	1876
Lee-Warner (Sir W.)	Protected Princes of India.	1894
Lowell (A. L.)	Governments and Parties in Continental Europe.	1896
Lyall (Sir A. C.)	Gazetteer for Haidarabad Assigned Districts.	1870
	Rise and Expansion of Brit. Dominion in India.	1894
Malleson (Col.)	History of the French in India.	1868
	Native States in India.	1875
	Final French Struggle in India.	1878
	Paper in Roy. Col. Institute Proceedings (Hyderabad).	1883
Marsham	H. of India.	1901
Pharaoh and Co.	Gazetteer of Southern India. (Madras.)	1855
Prinsep	H. of B. India (1813–1823).	1825
Rapson	Struggle between England and France for Supremacy in India. (Le Bas Prize Essay.)	1887

Authors		Editions
RUSSEL (H.)	A letter to the Court of Directors of the E. I. Co.	1822
SAMUELSON	India Past and Present.	1890
SEWELL (R.)	A Sketch of the dynasties of Southern India.	1883
SOHRABJI-JAHANGIR	Representative Men of India.	1889
TEMPLE (Sir R.)	Letter in "Correspondence regarding the comparative Merits of British and Native administration in India."	1867
	Journals kept in Hyderabad, etc.	1887
	Men and Events of my time, etc.	1882
THORNTON	Gen. Sir R. Meade and the Feudatory States of Central India.	1898
TUPPER	Our Indian Protectorate.	1893
WELLINGTON	Despatches, India, Vol. 2.	1844
WESTLAKE	Chapters on the Principles of International Law.	1894
WILKS	Historical Sketches of the South of India.	1810
Y.Z.	A seasonable letter on the late Treaty with the Nizam.	1768
OFFICIAL	Treaties (with the Nizam) 1759–1853.	

AUTHORITIES (*continued*).

PERIODICAL PUBLICATIONS.

Annales de l'École libre des Sciences Politiques, 1899.
Asiatic Quarterly Review, vol. 7, 1893–1894 (page 59).
„ „ „ vol. 8, 1894 (p. 36).
„ „ „ vol. 10, 1895 (pp. 312–344).
Calcutta Review, vol. 11.
„ „ vol. 100.
Fortnightly Review, 1897.
Madras „ vol. 4, 1898.
Quarterly „ vol. 104.
Westminster „ Jan. 1863.

CAMBRIDGE: PRINTED BY J. AND C. F. CLAY, AT THE UNIVERSITY PRESS.

NIZAM

ASAF JAH DYNASTY

COAT OF ARMS, OF ASAF JAH DYNASTY

The Nizam-ul-Mulk of Hyderabad, popularly known as the Nizam of Hyderabad, was a monarch of the Hyderabad State, now divided into Telangana state, Hyderabad-Karnataka region of Karnataka and Marathwada region of Maharashtra. Nizam, shortened from Nizam-ul-Mulk, meaning Administrator of the Realm, the title of the sovereigns of Hyderabad State, was the premier Prince of India, since 1724, belonging to the Asaf Jah dynasty.

The ***Asaf Jah Dynasty*** **was founded by** ***Mir Qamar-ud-Din Siddiqi***, a viceroy of the Deccan under the Mughal Empire from 1713 to 1721. He intermittently ruled after Aurangzeb's death in 1707. In 1724, Mughal control lapsed, and Asaf Jah declared himself independent in Hyderabad.

NIZAM

1

Nizam-ul-Mulk, Asaf Jah I

Mir Qamar-ud-din Khan

Nizam From:

July 31, 1724 - June 1, 1748

Nizam-ul-Mulk, Asaf Jah I

Mir Qamar-ud-din Khan

(August 20, 1671 – June 1, 1748)

NIZAM

1

Nizam-ul-Mulk, Asaf Jah I

Mir Qamar-ud-din Khan

Mir Qamar-ud-din Khan Siddiqi Bayafandi (20 August 1671 – 1 June 1748) was a Turkic nobleman with some Arab ancestry and the founder of the Asaf Jahi dynasty. He established the Hyderabad state, and ruled it from 1724 to 1748. He is also known by his titles Chin Qilich Khan (awarded by emperor Aurangzeb in 1690–91), Nizam-ul-Mulk (awarded by Farrukhsiyar in 1713) and Asaf Jah (awarded by Muhammad Shah in 1725).

According to his contemporary Shah Waliullah and the British historian Henry George Briggs, Asaf Jah I was the most influential man in the Indian Subcontinent after the death of Aurangzeb.

Early Life:

He was born to Ghazi ud-Din Khan Siddiqi Feroze Jung I and his first wife Wazir un-nisa Begum at Agra on 20 August 1671 as Mir Qamar ud-din Khan Siddiqi. The name was given to him by the Mughal Emperor Aurangazeb. His paternal and maternal grandparents were both important Mughal generals and courtiers namely; Qilich Khan II (Paternal) and Jumlat-ul-Mulk Allami Sa'adullah Khan (Maternal), the Vizier of Emperor Shah Jahan. He was educated privately. At the age of six, Mir Qamar-ud-din Khan accompanied his father to the Mughal court in 1677. Emperor Aurangzeb awarded him a Mansab.

Loyalty to Aurangzeb:

Mir Qamar-ud-din Khan displayed considerable skill as a warrior and before he reached his teens began accompanying his father into battle. In 1688 aged 17 he joined his father in the successful assault on the fort of Adoni and was promoted to the rank of 2000 zat and 500 horse and presented with the finest Arab steed with gold trappings and a pastille perfumed with ambergris from the Mughal court.

At the age of nineteen, the Emperor bestowed on him the title "Chin Fateh Khan". He was also gifted a female elephant and at age 20 he was bestowed with the title of "Chin Qilich Khan" (boy swordsman) for surviving an attack that blew off three of his horse's legs during the Siege of Wagingera Fort. For fighting on and capturing the fort he was raised to rank of 5000 horse and awarded 15 million dams, a jeweled sabre and a third elephant.

At 26, he was appointed Commander in Chief and Viceroy, first in Bijapur, then Malwa and later of the Deccan.

He inherited his family's military prowess. Henry George Briggs, a historian, wrote "If Moosulman were accustomed to perpetuate the memory of their heroes by posthumous ovations, India might have seen a hundred statues of her greatest Mohammedan hero of the eighteenth century".

Life after Aurangzeb:

After Aurangzeb's death he was appointed Governor of Oudh. After Bahadur Shah's (Muazzam Shah i Alam Bahadur Shah the 1st) death he opted for a private life in Delhi. His sabbatical was cut short when in 1712 the sixth of Aurangzeb's successors, Farrukhsiyar son of Azeem Ush Shaan convinced him to take up the post of Viceroy of the Deccan with the title of Nizam ul-Mulk (Regulator of the Realm) Fateh Jung.

His enemies accuse Nizam ul-Mulk of building his own power-base independently of the Mughals in Delhi, while continuing to give obeisance to the throne and even remitting money to the centre. He was then called upon by Farrukhsiyar to help fight off the Sayyid Brothers. Farrukhsiyar lost his strife against the Saadaat i Baarha Sayyid Brothers and was killed.

Vizier of the Mughal Sultanate:

Later Nizam ul-Mulk was rewarded for defeating the Saiyyid Brothers with the post of Vizier in the court of Muhammad Shah, the 18-year-old successor.

But all did not work as planned. Nizam ul-Mulk's attempts to reform the corrupt Mughal administration with its cliques of concubines and eunuchs created many enemies. According to his biographer, Yusuf Husain, he grew to hate the "harlots and jesters" who were the Emperor's constant companions and greeted all great nobles of the realm with lewd gestures and offensive epithets. Nizam ul-Mulk's desire to restore the etiquette of the Court and the discipline of the State to the standard of Shah Jahan's time earned him few friends. The courtiers poisoned the mind of the Emperor against him.

Asaf Jah I, Viceroy of the Deccan

In 1724 Nizam ul-Mulk resigned his post in disgust and set off for the Deccan to resume the Vice-royalty, only to find Mubariz Khan, who had been appointed governor by Emperor Farrukhsiyar nine years earlier, refusing to vacate the post. Mubariz Khan had successfully restored law and order in the Deccan but he was also loyal to the Mughal throne making only token payments and dividing plum administrative posts among his sons, his uncle and his favourite slave eunuchs. Unimpressed by the up-start occupying what he considered to be his rightful place, Nizam ul-Mulk gathered his forces at Shakarkhelda in Berar for a showdown with Mubariz Khan's army. The encounter was short but decisive. Wrapped in his bloodsoaked shawl, Mubariz Khan drove his war elephant into battle until he died from his wounds. His severed head was then sent to Delhi as proof of Nizam ul-Mulk's determination to annihilate anyone who stood in his way.

Asaf Jah I, Viceroy of the Deccan

Now came from the Emperor an elephant, jewels and the title of Asaf Jah, with directions to settle the country, repress the turbulent, punish the rebels and cherish the people. Asaf Jah, or the one equal to Asaf, the Grand Vizier in the court of King Solomon, was the highest title that could be awarded to a subject of the Mughal Empire. There were no lavish ceremonies to mark the establishment of the Asaf Jahi dynasty in 1724. The inauguration of the first Nizam took place behind closed doors in a private ceremony attended by the new ruler's closest advisors. Nizam ul-Mulk never formally declared his independence and insisted that his rule was entirely based on the trust reposed in him by the Mughal Emperor.

The Nizams had no throne, no crown and no symbol of sovereignty. Coins were minted with the Emperor's name until 1858. It was in the name of the Mughal ruler and not the Nizam that prayers were read out in the Friday Sermon. Qamaruddin Khan Siddiqi was essentially the servant of the Mughal Emperors.

As the Viceroy of the Deccan, the Nizam was the head of the executive and judicial departments and the source of all civil and military authority of the Mughal empire in the Deccan. All officials were appointed by him directly or in his name. Assisted by a Diwan the Nizam drafted his own laws, raised his own armies, flew his own flag and formed his own government.

Acknowledging Muhammad Shah's farman, Nizam ul-mulk had good reason to be grateful. Alongside his own personal wealth came the spoils of war and status, he was also entitled to the lion's share of gold unearthed in his dominions, the finest diamonds and gems from Golconda mines and the income from his vast personal estates.

He then divided his newly acquired kingdom into three parts. One third became his own private estate known as the Sarf-i-Khas, one third was allotted for the expenses of the government and was known as the Diwans territory, and the remainder was distributed to Muslim nobles (Jagirdar, Zamindars, Deshmukh), who in return paid nazars (gifts) to the Nizam for the privilege of collecting revenue from the villages under their suzerainty. The most important of these were the

Paigah estates. The Paigah's doubled up as generals, making it easy to raise an army should the Nizams Dominions come under attack. They were the equivalent to the Barmakids for the Abbasid Caliphate. Only second to the Nizams family, they were very important in the running of the government and even today their legacy lingers on with ruined palaces and tombs dotted around the once very feudal city of Hyderabad. On the sanads (scrolls) granting them their lands, inscribed in Persian were the words "as long as the Sun and the Moon are in rotation". The owners of the estates were mostly absentee landlords who cared little for the condition of the lands under their control. Jagirs were usually split into numerous pieces in order to prevent the most powerful of the nobles from entertaining any thought of carving out an empire for themselves. The system, which continued relatively unchanged until 1950, ensured a steady source of income for the state treasury and the Nizam himself.

Usage of War elephants:

A Mahout and its rider in service of the Mughal Emperor Muhammad Shah.

During a campaign against the Maratha in the year 1730, Nizam-ul-Mulk had no less than 1026 War elephants, 225 of which were armoured.

Nader Shah:

In 1738, From beyond the Hindu kush, Nader Shah started advancing towards Delhi through Afghanistan and the Punjab.

Nizam ul-Mulk sent his troops to Karnal, where Mughal Emperor Muhammed Shah's forces had gathered to turn back the Persian army. But the combined forces were cannon fodder for the Persian cavalry and its superior weaponry and tactics. Nader Shah defeated the combined armies of Muhammed Shah and the Nizam.

Nader Shah entered Delhi and stationed his troops there. Some locals of Delhi had a quarrel and attacked his soldiers. At this, Nader Shah flew into a rage, drew out his sword from the scabbard and ordered the City to be looted and ransacked. Muhammad Shah was unable to prevent Delhi from being destroyed.

When Nader Shah ordered the massacre in Delhi, neither the helpless Mughal Emperor Muhammed Shah nor any of his Ministers had the courage to speak to Nader Shah and negotiate for truce.

Only Asif Jah came forward and risked his life for by going to Nader Shah and asking him to end the bloodbath of the city. Legend has it that Asif Jah said to Nader Shah "You have taken the lifes of thousands of people of the city, if you still wish to continue the bloodshed, then bring those dead back to life and then kill them again, for there are none left to be killed". These words had a tremendous impact on Nader Shah - he immediately put his sword inside its scabbard, ended the massacre and returned to Persia.

Later life:

The Nizam was well suited to rule his own territory.The administration was under control.

In March 1742, the British who were based in Fort St George in Madras sent a modest hamper to Nizam ul-mulk in recognition of his leadership of the most important of the Mughal successor states. Its contents included a gold throne, gold and silver threaded silk from Europe, two pairs of large painted looking glasses, and equipage for coffee cups, 163.75 yards of green and 73.5 yards of crimson velvet, brocades, Persian carpets, a gold ceremonial cloth, two Arab horses, half a dozen ornate rose-water bottles and 39.75 chests of rose water – enough to keep the Nizam and his entire darbar fragrant for the rest of his reign. In return, the Nizam sent one horse, a piece of jewelery and a note warning the British that they had no right to mint their own currency, to which they complied.

It was after Nizam ul-mulk's death that his son and grandson sought help from the British and French in order to win the throne. Just days before he died in 1748, Asaf Jah dictated his last will and testament. The 17 clause document was a blueprint for governance and personal conduct that ranged from advice on how to keep the troops happy and well fed to an apology for neglecting his wife. He then reminded his successors to remain subservient to the Mughal Emperor who had granted them their office and rank. He warned against declaring war unnecessarily, but if forced to do so to seek the help of elders and saints and follow the sayings and practices of the Prophet. Finally, he insisted to his sons that "you must not lend your ears to tittle-tattle of the backbiters and slanderers, nor suffer the riff-raff to approach your presence."

Legacy:

Nizam-ul-Mulk is remembered as laying the foundation for what would become one of the most important Muslim states outside the Middle East by the first half of the twentieth century. Hyderabad state survived right through the period of British rule up to the time of Indian independence 1947, and was indeed the largest – the state covered an extensive 95,337 sq. miles, an area larger than Mysore or Gwalior and the size of Nepal and Kashmir put together (although it was the size of France when the first Nizam held reign) – and one of the most prosperous, among the princely states of the British Raj. The titles of "Nizam Ul Mulk" and "Asaf Jah" that were bestowed on him by the Mughal Emperors, carried his legacy as his descendants ruled under the title of " Nizam of Hyderabad" and the dynasty itself came to be known as the Asaf Jahi Dynasty.

By the Reign of the seventh Nizam, his dominion were similar in size to Belgium, but it was a far cry from when the first Nizam had ruled over a territory the size of France.

Death:

Nizam ul-mulk died aged 76. He died at Burhanpur, 1 June 1748 and was buried at mazaar of Shaikh Burhan ud-din Gharib Chisti, Khuldabad, near Aurangabad, where Aurangazeb is also buried.

Titles:

- 1685 : Khan
- 1691 : Khan Bahadur
- 1697 : Chin Qilich Khan (by Emperor Aurangazeb)
- 9 December 1707 : Khan-i-Dauran Bahadur
- 1712 : Ghazi ud-din Khan Bahadur and Firuz Jang
- 12 January 1713 : Khan-i-Khanan, Nizam ul-Mulk and Fateh Jang (by Emperor Farukh Siar)

- 12 July 1737 : Asaf Jah (by Emperor Muhammad Shah)
- 26 February 1739 : Amir ul-Umara and Bakshi ul-Mamalik (Paymaster-General)

Positions:

- 1701–1705 : Faujdar of the Carnatic and Talikota
- 1705–1706 : Faujdar of the Bijapur, Azamnagar and Belgaum
- 1706–1707 : Faujdar of Raichur, Talikota, Sakkhar and Badkal
- 1707 : Faujdar of Firoznagar and Balkona
- 9 December 1707 – 6 February 1711 : Subedar of Oudh and Faujdar of Gorakhpur
- 12 January 1713 – April 1715 : Subedar of the Deccan and Faujdar of the Carnatic

- April 1717 - 7 January 1719 : Faujdar of Moradabad
- 7 February-15 March 1719: Subedar of Patna
- 15 March 1719 – 1724 : Subedar of Malwa
- 1722–1724 : Subedar of Gujarat

FEEDBACK

Now that you have read the book ...

Was it interesting?

Did you enjoy what you wanted to read?
Was there any room for improvement?

Let us know at:

http://www.diamondbooks.ca/feedback

Your feedback is highly appreciated.

Thank you!

27440301R00074

Printed in Great Britain
by Amazon